Creating Great Visitor Experiences

A Guide for Museums, Parks, Zoos, Gardens, & Libraries

An experienceology® Guide

This is the first in a planned series of handbooks applying the eight-step Experience*ology* process to a variety of businesses. Other books will be targeted to 1) business owners in the retail, hospitality, and service fields, 2) health-care providers, 3) special events, travel, and trade shows, and possibly 4) Web sites.

Visit www.experienceology.com for updates on future books.

Creating Great Visitor Experiences

A Guide for Museums, Parks, Zoos, Gardens, & Libraries

Stephanie Weaver

Left Coast
Press Inc.

Walnut Creek, California

Left Coast Press Inc.

LEFT COAST PRESS, INC.
1630 North Main Street, #400
Walnut Creek, CA 94596
www.LCoastPress.com

ISBN 978-1-59874-168-1 hardcover
ISBN 978-1-59874-169-8 paperback

Library of Congress Cataloging-in-Publication Data
Weaver, Stephanie, 1961–

    Creating great vistor experiences : a guide for museums, parks, zoos, gardens & libraries / Stephanie Weaver.

    p. cm.

    Includes bibliographical references and index.

    ISBN-13: 978-1-59874-168-1 (hardback : alk. paper)

    ISBN-10: 1-59874-168-3 (hardback : alk. paper)

    ISBN-13: 978-1-59874-169-8 (pbk. : alk. paper)

    ISBN-10: 1-59874-169-1 (pbk. : alk. paper)

    1. Museum visitors--United States--Handbooks, manuals, etc. 2. Museum attendance--United States --Handbooks, manuals, etc. 3. Museums--Public relations--United States--Handbooks, manuals, etc. 4. Museums--United States--Management--Handbooks, manuals, etc. 5. Parks--Public use--United States--Handbooks, manuals, etc. 6. Zoo visitors--United States--Handbooks, manuals, etc. 7. Library users--United States--Handbooks, manuals, etc. 8. Public relations--United States--Handbooks, manuals, etc. I. Title.

AM11.W43 2007

069'.1--dc22

2007004412

Printed in the United States of America

The paper used in this publication meets the minimum requirements of American National Standard for Information Sciences—Permanence of Paper for Printed Library Materials, ANSI/NISO Z39.48–1992.

08 09 10 11   5 4 3

CONTENTS

DEDICATION

For everyone who works more than
a forty-hour week, making less than
they could, because they believe in
what they're doing.

For every institution with small resources
and a big mission that's trying to
compete with for-profit destinations.

May this book inspire you and help
level the playing field.

The need for change

CHAPTER 1

Competing in an experience-driven world

Life is a series of experiences—some we want to repeat, and some we'd like to forget. Perhaps things like this have happened to you:

- You walked wearily through an endless hall in a natural-history museum, searching in vain for a bench.
- You were having a great time at an art museum's restaurant—you got wonderful food and warm service in a fun atmosphere—and then you found a dirty bathroom with a cracked, drippy sink.
- A salesclerk's sour attitude ruined your experience in a national park store, even though they had fantastic merchandise.
- Or maybe you sat down at a computer in a library to find a grimy keyboard and a sticky mouse.

Creating Great Visitor Experiences will help you sidestep pitfalls like these and instead create high-quality experiences that your visitors want to repeat. Your visitors have many other ways to spend their leisure time, so your experience must be unique and enjoyable. The nonprofit world is not immune to competition; getting and holding an audience is critical to a museum, park, or zoo's financial health. Because people have so many choices, your site has to stand out from the pack by providing a sophisticated, meaningful, and memorable experience. The way to set yourself apart is to understand that, while you are a nonprofit, you are also in the business of creating and selling cultural experiences.[1]

This book takes you step by step through the process of cultivating and maintaining the highest level of visitor satisfaction. I coined the term "Experience*ology*"® to describe my approach, which combines elements of art, science, and common sense. Experience*ology* can be used to improve the quality of visitors' experiences at any museum, park, science center, living-history site, garden, zoo, aquarium, or library.

Experience adds up

A good visitor experience helps you in two critical ways. First, since your goal is educating the public and serving your community, a positive experience supports learning. By helping to save and make you money, a good experience brings in additional revenue that can be used for public programs and other services.[2]

Second, a crafted experience increases your potential for earning and generating revenue, allowing you to remain financially viable for years to come.[3] If you're providing a poor visitor experience, your organization is probably suffering financially in some way. On the other hand, providing good experiences saves you money in advertising and promotion, because it costs five times more to attract a new visitor than it does to keep one you already have.[4] In addition, a good Web site is part of the cost benefit of the well-crafted experience; it saves and makes you money by reducing customer-service telephone hours, as visitors can easily use it to renew services, buy products, and get directions on their own.[5]

It costs five times more to attract a new visitor than to keep one you already have.

Why you need this book

To court your visitors
To improve your site

This book is intended for any informal learning site that serves the public. Experience*ology* applies to all kinds of museums and similar places. I will call the people who come through your doors "visitors" to keep it simple. At your institution you might call them guests, users, or patrons. I'll use the term "site" to describe your place of business. You might call it your museum, institution, park, heritage site, garden, library, or facility. Don't let the language get in the way.

After reading this book, you may decide to choose another term to describe your visitors. To some, the term "visitor" sets up an "us vs. them" mentality from the start, as they are only visiting your site. Some sites now prefer "guest," a word most commonly used in the hospitality industry. "Patrons" is an old-fashioned library word that no longer reflects today's service-oriented libraries. And "users" has an unfortunate association with drugs. Whatever term you choose, it's your attitude toward your visitors that counts, but I'll show you a few examples of how changing terminology can reflect a more visitor-centered approach.

Throughout this book we'll look at examples from a variety of museums and other businesses around the world. Some will be very similar to your own, others very different. All of them will give you ideas about how—and how not—to provide great experiences for your visitors.

From an education advocate to an experience advocate

I've spent my career at the intersection between art and science. My background in film and design, combined with a degree in health education, gave me a unique perspective on nonprofit sites' educational roles. Over the years I have acted as a liaison between content experts—doctors, botanists, or scientists—and the public. I view myself as a translator, someone who distills the essence of material down into tasty bites of (correct) information that the public will enjoy. Over the years I've been a passionate advocate for education and interpretation at the sites where I've worked.

In 2002 I was invited to Brookfield Zoo in Illinois for a conference on conservation psychology. We held spirited debates over how to change visitor behavior at our conservation-minded institutions, with the focus on how we could make a difference on pressing global environmental issues. And then Robert Bixler, a professor in recreation studies, stood up. "Recreation is not the enemy! Recreation sounds frivolous," he said. "But playing in natural environments is key to caring about them. It's good for people to have pleasant experiences at zoos and parks." While we all laughed, his impassioned defense of enjoyment struck a chord with me. Since then, Richard Louv has made a similar argument in his book *Last Child in the Woods*.[6]

While still at the conference, I thought back to the project I'd recently completed, a database of the interpretive signs at the San Diego Zoo—*more than a thousand* messages. I thought about the long fight to install a sign about the African bushmeat crisis next to the beautiful gorilla habitat. For the first time I wondered, were we right to place that stark message in that location? Was that the best way to reach people?

What exactly were we trying to accomplish in the long run? How did interpretation fit into the bigger picture?

I was reading two books at the time, *The Experience Economy*[7] and *Why We Buy*.[8] The first book pinpointed what was bothering me about focusing solely on interpretation. If visitors were having a lousy time in the parking lot, or at ticketing, or they couldn't find a bathroom, then all the time, money, and effort we spent on interpretation was, possibly, wasted. It was a horrible thought. If visitors were spending from two to four hours at the zoo, how many signs was it reasonable to expect them to read? Ten percent of the total? Twenty percent? I never once considered how many messages there were when I added new ones. We had nearly two thousand signs on the grounds, if you counted donor-recognition, wayfinding, cautionary, and merchandising messages. That's a *lot* of reading. We had never talked about how much time visitors were spending overall at the site, nor had we designed the experience as a whole and integrated signage into it. I was pretty sure that this was the case at most museums, too.

As I read *Why We Buy*, I wondered whether anyone had taken Underhill's twenty-five years of experience tracking retail customers and applied it to museums. People are people, and behavior is behavior. The book was chock full of useful tidbits that museums could put into practice. I wasn't the only person thinking this way; I found a paper written by Robert Webb for the Visitor Studies Association in 1993; Webb argued that consumer research, which was plentiful, could be applied to help museums in their design and messaging.

All leisure destinations, museums included, were negatively impacted by 9/11, when people stopped traveling. This compounded the challenge nonprofits were already facing with the explosion of leisure-time competition in the 1990s. I wondered whether there were resources available outside the museum field that could help museums compete while allowing them to remain true to their mission. I began working to develop a process that could help a variety of sites analyze their overall visitor experience. In 2004 I presented my eight-step process as a workshop at the California Association of Museums conference. The enthusiastic response encouraged me to write this book, so that even museums with few resources could apply this information to improve their visitors' experiences. No one has the money to rebuild and redesign a museum from the ground up, but with more attention to detail and more thought about what visitors want, sites can create a great experience that many will want to repeat. My "evolution" mirrored what was happening in our culture as well.

The evolution of experiences

Do you remember your first cappuccino? Mine—rich, foamy, and exotic—must have been at a good Italian restaurant in Chicago. The next one I drank was at a neighborhood coffeehouse, when coffeehouses were still rare. And then suddenly it seemed that, overnight, there was a Starbucks on every corner. Starbucks founder Howard Schultz got his inspiration in the coffeehouses of Milan.[9] Before the Starbucks phenomenon, coffee was something you got in a can at the grocery store, or was slopped into a chipped beige cup at a diner. Starbucks took a fifty-cent cup of coffee, added foam and a logo, and sold it for $2.95. Why do we pay $3 for a cup of coffee? Starbucks is all about the experience: the names of the drinks, that distinctive *whoosh* of the steamer, the "baristas" who write your name on the cup. Every aspect of Starbucks' performance has been designed to create this effect; none of it is accidental. Starbucks offers a consistent experience worldwide. On a brutally hot day in Hong Kong, my fellow travelers and I pounced upon a Starbucks and fell gratefully into the familiar chairs, sucking down Frappuccinos as we recovered from our trip up Victoria Peak. Never has an experience tasted so good. If you haven't ever thought about what makes Starbucks work, try to imagine applying some of their techniques for creating experience to your site. How can you easily customize the experience? How can you add sights, sounds, and scents? Is your experience consistently good?

While Starbucks has capitalized on people's desire for experiences, Howard Schultz didn't invent the experience business or fanatical attention to detail. That honor goes to Walt Disney.[10] Everyone on the staff at Disney theme parks is aware of being in the experience business; all the employees (even the ones who work at the on-site zoo) are called cast members. Every aspect of the site is carefully arranged to create a particular mood, feeling, and outcome.[11] (In an artfully designed rustic area at Disney's Animal Kingdom in Florida, I noticed a large asphalt patch on the ground in the shape of . . . mouse ears.) Other companies

Author Seth Godin calls this attention to detail "vernacular" and sees all these details as coloring in the story you are trying to tell.

have followed Disney's example, transforming traditional businesses into experience businesses with great success. Author Seth Godin calls this attention to detail "vernacular" and sees all these details as coloring in the story you are trying to tell.[12]

The Nordstrom department store chain began as a shoe store in the Pacific Northwest. Nordstrom prides itself on being able to fit anyone, even people with two different-size feet. Shoes are so important to Nordstrom that they analyzed what prevented people from buying shoes and made changes accordingly. They had special chairs designed, with high seats, firm upholstery, and sturdy arms. This allows a customer to sit comfortably while he is being fitted and to push himself up easily to try out the shoes he's chosen.[13] Nordstrom also provides live piano music, thick, soft carpeting, and legendary customer service. The chain has been highly profitable, and they've successfully turned the everyday act of buying shoes into something memorable. What is as critical to you in your visitor experience as shoes are to Nordstrom? If you have places where people sit a lot, have you considered special chairs? Have you thought about any obstacles there are to getting people to engage in your content, and then redesigned your experience to remove them?

Southwest Airlines has seen thirty years of profitability in the competitive and unstable airline industry. They've done it with a combination of quick flight turnarounds (that's why they don't reserve seats), flight attendants in polo shirts and khaki shorts who joke over the P.A. system, and consistent customer service.[14] Southwest changed the flying paradigm profoundly, by taking a stodgy, rigid system and rethinking it from the customer's point of view. Is there anything rigid about the way you do business? How about taking a fresh look at everything you do from your visitor's perspective?

Your competition is everywhere

In order to compete, you need to understand how the experience trend relates to your site. Competition for your visitors' leisure time is intense. Restaurants have morphed into themed entertainment venues based on movies (The Bubba Gump Shrimp Company), products (Weber Grill Restaurants),[15] or even cable television channels (The ESPN Zone). When you were a kid, there were no virtual-reality arcades, twenty-four-hour gaming centers complete with shower facilities,[16] paintball centers, or rock-climbing walls at the mall. Even in the nonprofit world, things have changed. Park rangers are asked to wrap educational messages inside "pleasurable experiences."[17] Museum curators used to consider their work a higher calling, above mere entertainment.[18] But, whether we like it or not, the Zagat Survey now publishes a family guide that rates museums alongside for-profit entertainment destinations.[19]

Some museums are flourishing on this leveled playing field, with a few making the Zagat Top 10 for child appeal. But others are having trouble challenging their for-profit competition. Despite an ideal location on Chicago's Michigan Avenue, the Terra Museum of American Art closed late in 2004. Across the street, Niketown is thriving. In Washington, D.C., even the free museums of the Smithsonian Institution have seen attendance drop.[20] In Atlanta the prestigious High Museum of Art draws fewer annual visitors than the World of Coca-Cola pavilion.[21] Perhaps it's coincidental, but the High Museum has recently announced a three-year partnership with the Louvre. The arrangement will bring legendary art treasures from Paris to Atlanta,[22] and the High's appeal as a visitor experience will almost certainly increase.

Your experience can set you apart

Accountants look at business in terms of the bottom line—expenses vs. profit. On a day-to-day basis you might focus on the prices you offer—your admission fee, your summer camp tuition rate, or what you charge for a T-shirt in your shop. While museums don't normally think of their admission prices as market driven, it's true that competitive prices do draw a certain number of visitors, and prices that are too high can limit attendance. But truly extraordinary customer service could make an increased admission fee work. If you revamped every aspect of your business to be memorable and engaging from start to finish, you'd likely see a greater flow of visitors who visit more often and spend more money. While every museum is unique, and we don't like to think of ourselves as competing with soccer or the mall, visitors *are* making the choice to visit us instead of another venue, a venue that may be for profit. Crafting a great experience for your visitors is the key element to setting yourself apart from all the other choices.

Bad experiences crush your bottom line

What you should fear most: a visitor who has a bad time at your facility. How much difference does a bad experience make? Here are some ways that a poor visitor experience might result in lost income:

- You sell an expensive toy to a visitor in your gift shop. During the sale, the clerk is rude. Later, when the toy malfunctions, the visitor promptly returns it to you and buys a cheaper replacement on amazon.com.

- A family has trouble finding a bathroom during their visit to your historical museum, and the atmosphere doesn't feel child friendly. When they receive your membership notice in the mail, they decide to try someplace new.

- You have great attendance during a special event at your garden festival, but an older couple has a bad time with the crowds, the lines, and the rushed restaurant servers. They don't come back the next month, or even the next year.

- A visitor is buying a membership on your Web site, but the site is so slow and confusing that he abandons his shopping cart. If he wants the membership badly enough, he calls your customer-service line. Frustrated, he might decide to buy a Sea World membership instead. Either way, you have lost money, as your visitor-service rep has to fix a problem your Web site created.[23]

People love to complain about their bad experiences, and they will tell an average of ten other people about their problem with you.[24] You may never even hear about it directly, because only one of every twenty-seven visitors actually takes a complaint to the source of the problem.[25] And with the Internet, complaints posted on sites like YouTube last forever. However good your museum, you can't afford that kind of negative publicity. Experience*ology* will help you create positive word-of-mouth advertising, as your visitors tell their friends about the great time they had with you.

How the book is organized

Creating Great Visitor Experiences will help you make the most of your site with the resources you have available. You don't have to spend a fortune to make everything shiny and new. You do need to look at every aspect of your site through your visitor's eyes. The exercises for Chapter 1 are on page 155, where you can rate your current strengths and weaknesses. In Chapter 2 I'll define "visitor experience," a term that means different things to different people. That will conclude **Section 1: The need for change.**

Section 2: Your visitors and your staff, includes what visitors may want from your site, how to influence them in your favor, how your brand identity shapes their experiences, and how to empower your staff to create great experiences on a daily basis.

Section 3: Your site, covers each of the eight steps to a crafted visitor experience in detail, tracking a visit from start to finish. The steps are invitation, welcome, orientation, comfort, communication, sensation, common sense, and finale.

Section 4: How to use this book, contains exercises keyed to each chapter. These will help you apply the content to your site, so that you can make Experience*ology* come alive. With each chapter summary I've highlighted some helpful sections of other books or Web sites you may want to explore in order to delve more deeply into a topic. You'll also find detailed suggestions for using this book in a timeframe that suits your needs.

Read through the whole book first, and then decide which exercises apply best to your site. If you want to get started with exercises right away, the instructions on page 139 explain how. This is a practical, how-to book. As you work through it, you'll identify what needs changing, brainstorm ideas and creative solutions, and set priorities. There is no fixed cost for this process. The amount of money you spend depends on you: your goals, time, staff, and budget.

You can use this book to launch a complete overhaul or to tweak an already great experience. You might want to focus on just one of the eight steps, or to apply each of them sequentially. The process will work for small sites with one staff person and huge sites with multimillion-dollar budgets. Welcome to Experience*ology*!

The Eight Steps:
1. Invitation
2. Welcome
3. Orientation
4. Comfort
5. Communication
6. Sensation
7. Common sense
8. Finale

CHAPTER 2

The bear on the bicycle: the visitor experience defined

There are two dimensions to the visitor experience; think of them as inside and outside.

- **Inside.** First, the experience happens in your visitors' perceptions. It's seen from their point of view, created by a combination of their feelings, sensations, and prior experiences. Unfortunately, what you intend doesn't always matter. All that counts is what's happening inside a visitor on the day she's at your site. You can't control this inside dimension. No two visitors will ever have the same experience, since everyone has a unique point of view.[1]

- **Outside.** Second, an experience is made up of many separate pieces outside the visitor. That's your part. The outside dimension begins the instant a person decides to visit, continues throughout her time with you, and ends when she leaves. You control nearly every aspect of this outside dimension. I've divided a visit into eight sequential steps, allowing you to examine each of them in detail in a logical order while you imagine your visitor experiencing them.

Eight steps to a crafted visitor experience

1. Invitation

The invitation step begins when a potential visitor says, "Let's do something today." It ends when she arrives in your parking lot and spies your front door.

2. Welcome

The welcome step begins at your entrance and ends when the visitor has had contact with someone who works for you.

3. Orientation

When the visitor moves away from your greeter, the orientation step begins. It ends when she decides what to do first.

4. Comfort

The comfort step is found throughout your site. It's designed in—to permanent structures, built-ins, seating, exhibits or displays, and signs.

5. Communication

Everything you convey in written or spoken words is included in the communication step.

6. Sensation

When you're designing your experience or setting up visitors' interaction with your staff, always remember to ask, "Is it fun?" "Does it engage all five senses?" and "Is it unexpected?"

7. Common sense

The common-sense step provides smarter, more logical, more efficient ways to run your business. It includes using visitor studies, applying trends, realigning your mission if necessary, and collaborating with like-minded organizations.

8. Finale

The finale is everything a visitor leaves with, both tangible and intangible.

Now for the bear on the bike

I once worked at a children's museum on the upper level of a mall. Directly opposite our entrance was a toy store, which had set up a tightrope in the small atrium between us so that a mechanical toy bear could bicycle back and forth. We got complaints from museum visitors when the bear was gone, and it took us a while to figure out what people were talking about, since none of us could locate a bear within our museum! We found that a highlight of many kids' visits had been watching that aerial act; people didn't make a distinction between the toy store and our site; it was all part of their experience. While we didn't have control over the bear, it helped us realize that our visitors' experience didn't start at our front door.

Your site, from the moon

To understand your visitor experience, you have to take a giant step back from your site, as if you were viewing the earth from the moon. How does your site compare to all the other sites of its type, all the other leisure destinations in town, all the other offerings on your street? You will need to examine details you might normally overlook: the exterior of your building, your signs, your staff, your bathrooms.[2] Look at your business while sales are being rung up, as people are browsing exhibits, when they are waiting in line, as they are greeted. Look at your paint, your cabinets, your walls, and your parking lot. Look at the intangible aspects of the experience, too. How does it feel to walk into your site? How does it feel when you leave? Do you want to come back?

Your brand *is* your experience. When you look at the big picture, it makes sense that your marketing, public relations, advertising, Web site, any special programs you offer, and staff training all support a great visitor experience. This is how the marketing concept of creating a brand relates to your experience. You can't separate them; your brand is only as good as the poorest piece of your experience: a sour reception, a smelly bathroom, a confusing map. We'll talk in detail about creating your brand in Chapter 5. The more consistent and integrated the experience you offer, the stronger your brand will be. Great experiences engage your visitor, tell a story, and fit all the pieces of a visit together to create a positive memory.

A Chinese field of dreams

There are quite a few museums in the Sichuan province of China. Many that I've visited featured bad taxidermy: endangered clouded leopards and giant pandas forever frozen with grimaces on their faces. So my expectations weren't high on the last day of a tour when our group arrived at the San Xing Dui Archeology Museum, smack in the middle of acres of farmland outside Chengdu, the capital of Sichuan.

As we walked toward the entrance, the parking lot and building swam in the thick, humid air. Refreshing, cool darkness greeted us as we entered, and when our eyes adjusted, we saw a stunning sight. A golden tower—a replica of a tree-of-life sculpture two and a half stories tall—stands in the center of a space that spirals up around it. The

San Xing Dui Museum documents the bronze age of the Shu Dynasty. Before the treasures were discovered, the Shu Dynasty was thought to be a mythical part of China's early heritage. Then in the 1980s farmers happened to dig up pits full of bronzes, and a fabulous museum was built to showcase them. The Shu created bronze masks, some as small as your hand. A huge replica of a mask hangs at the top of each tall display case; beneath that a line drawing of the mask is positioned; and the actual object is spotlighted at eye level. When you walk into a gallery, you see a semicircle of huge masks, one after another. You stop to examine each one closely, appreciating its exquisite detail, which is highlighted by the drawing.

Even though there were very few signs in English, we spent several hours drinking it all in. The museum looks like it cost a fortune, with rich surfaces of lacquered metal. But closer examination revealed a clever use of wallpaper, carpeting, and laminates to create the illusion of luxury. In the gift shop at the top of the museum's spiral, I was delighted to find a spectacular reproduction of a mask, beautifully framed, to take home as a souvenir. When I got back to the ground-level gift shop near our bus, it was buzzing with activity. My fellow travelers, out of cash after two weeks on the road, had discovered that the shop accepted Visa and were loading up on memories themselves.

Your mission in life

Who is your visitor?
What do you want to accomplish?
Where is your community?

The first step in crafting a visitor experience, like the one I had at San Xing Dui, is to create a mission statement. Most nonprofits in the U.S. have them.[3] Your statement clarifies your core purpose, helping to create your brand story. Good mission statements include who you want to attract, what your purpose is, and which geographic area you serve.[4] You might start by asking, "Why do we exist? What would be missing for our visitors if we weren't around? If our collections were suddenly destroyed, would we close?"[5]

The Texas State Aquarium in Corpus Christi incorporates cooling water sculptures that mist the air, an entry walkway embedded with the shapes of swimming rays, and exhibits about life in and on the water.[6] Their experience brings to life their mission: "Inspiring appreciation and wise stewardship of the Gulf of Mexico."[7]

The exercise on page 157 will help you develop or refine a usable mission statement. You'll build on this foundation in later chapters as you design your crafted visitor experience. In the next chapter we'll examine some of the things your visitors will be looking for at your site.

Your visitors and your staff

CHAPTER 3

What do they want?

What are visitors looking for? A lot of very smart people have developed some theories you may find useful. While we don't always think of our visitors as "consumers," information originally applied to retail sales can be an important tool for helping you create the best possible visitor experiences.

Free time in America

Think of your visitors' free time as a precious commodity. Americans spend about three hours a day watching TV, forty-five minutes socializing, and twenty minutes doing some kind of sports, recreation, or other physical activity. At the bottom of the pile are the twelve minutes left for arts, culture, and entertainment. (Chores, shopping, and eating fill out the rest of the day.)[1] Nearly eight percent of Americans travel more than one hour to work, which again cuts into their available free time.[2]

From the Experience*ology* perspective, it's that three-hour chunk of television-viewing time that's most intriguing. If you want an hour from your visitor, you can go after his socializing + cultural time. If you want more active participation, go after his socializing + "sports" time. If you want more than two hours from him, go after his TV time.

What might get visitors to spend two hours with you instead of watching a reality show like *Fear Factor*? In the summertime in the U.S., longer days combined with reruns make television a less appealing choice than it is at other times of the year. The Museum of Contemporary Art in Los Angeles took advantage of long summer nights in 2005 and created a smash hit with its entertainment series *Night Vision*. The twelve consecutive Saturday nights featured live music, DJs, spoken-word performances, film screenings, and art-making booths until midnight.[3]

Six types of free-time rewards

Is there one magic thing visitors want from their free time? Researcher Marilyn Hood analyzed sixty years of leisure-time studies to find out.

Her results showed not one but six emotional rewards of free time:

- Social interaction
- Active participation
- Comfortable surroundings
- Challenging, new, or unusual experiences
- Opportunities to learn
- A sense of doing something worthwhile

As a museum researcher, Hood wanted to know why some people stay away from museums. Did the six rewards factor into their decision? She did a study for the Toledo Museum of Art in Ohio to find out why some people were visiting while others were staying away. Her results show the value of understanding visitors' motivations. They don't always match our assumptions.

Hood's study identified three groups of people in the Toledo area: those who visited the art museum regularly, those who were occasional visitors, and those who never visited. Regular attendees described the museum experience as offering them three rewards: the challenge of new experiences, opportunities for learning, and the feeling that the experience was worthwhile. Those who never came to the museum were looking for activities that offered them social interaction, an active role in programs or activities, and comfortable surroundings. They didn't think the museum could offer them those rewards. People who came to the museum only once or twice a year were more like the non-attendees in their attitudes. They usually came on family days or for special festivals, when they felt they'd be offered more chances to socialize and see performances. Being with their families and friends also helped the people who rarely visited feel comfortable in the museum environment. This was a surprise to museum staff members, who assumed that all their visitors valued the experience for the same reasons.[4]

So, people came to this art museum seeking more than one reward, Hood's study found. They didn't come just to learn, to socialize, or to buy a nice souvenir. People usually gave a combination of reasons. A more recent study found that Americans go to different types of venues seeking different rewards. For example, they might go to a museum to learn something new but attend a music performance to socialize.[5]

The four realms of experiences

We've learned that visitors can receive six different rewards from their leisure-time experiences. But are all leisure experiences equally valuable to the visitor? In their book *The Experience Economy*, Joseph Pine and James Gilmore describe four realms of experience that businesses offer:

- Educational
- Entertainment
- Esthetic
- Escapist[6]

Let's try out their theory in Balboa Park. The park, in the center of San Diego, was developed for the 1915 Panama-California International Exposition. With gorgeous historical buildings covered in ornate plaster carvings, it offers many fun ways to spend free time, including hiking, Frisbee golf, archery, lawn bowling, and a dozen museums to explore. Walking east across the Laurel Street Bridge, we come first to the San Diego Museum of Man.

- Educational

   The Museum of Man offers what Pine and Gilmore call an educational experience focused on anthropology and archeology; there are cool mummies, evolution exhibits, Mexican pottery, and Mayan carvings.

- Entertainment

   The Old Globe Theatre behind the Museum of Man offers an entertainment experience; a theatergoer sits back and enjoys the show.

- Esthetic

   The three art museums in the park are examples of esthetic experiences; here people can absorb and appreciate beautiful things.

- Escapist

   You can create your own escapist experiences at the Reuben H. Fleet Science Center—riding in motion-simulator machines, performing experiments, and playing science-based games.

Unique venues like those in Balboa Park offer a variety of experiences to visitors, and of course there is some overlap among sites. A single experience can blend escapist, educational, and esthetic qualities. The new public library in Cerritos, California, received an Expy Award in 2003 from Pine and Gilmore for the outstanding experience it offers visitors. Its Old World Reading Room with a holographic fireplace and an aquarium wall in the children's section are just two of its unique educational and entertainment features.[7] Outdoor experiences can be escapist and esthetic. To help participants focus on the esthetics of the environment, some river guides conduct a "silent float" on the last day of a rafting trip that many visitors recall as a magical interlude.[8]

People don't sit back to enjoy this show. For the last sixteen years, the Neo-Futurists have been creating an escapist theater experience in Chicago. Their show, *Too Much Light Makes the Baby Go Blind*, is billed as thirty plays in sixty minutes.[9] When you check in at the box office, you are given a crazy nametag and a list of the night's plays. You roll a die to determine your ticket price. Before the show begins, a cast member orders a pizza while the audience calls out the names of favorite toppings. A huge timer is set for sixty minutes, the show begins, and you shout out the number of the play you want to see first. Out of the darkness a cast member leaps up, pulls that number off a clothesline hanging above the stage, and yells the name of the play. One night the entire audience had to zoom down the stairs to watch a play set in the center lane of the street outside, then hoof it back upstairs for the next part of the show. At the end of the hour the timer goes off. Usually the performers finish all thirty plays in time, but you never know what to expect. At the end of the Sunday night performance the dice are rolled onstage one last time, and fate decides whether two or up to twelve new plays will be written for the following weekend. The pizza, cut into tiny squares, arrives and is put onstage for audience members to sample as they leave. It's a heady evening of entertainment, esthetics, and escape (with some aerobics thrown in). Perhaps your site could team up with a local theater company to create an engaging experience like this as a special event.

Making it work for you

Start thinking about whether your site is primarily educational, entertainment, esthetic, or escapist. As more for-profit businesses adopt museum techniques, it raises the level of expectation for museum visitors as well. In Chandler, Arizona, Dr. John Culp has created a unique dental office called Jungle Roots Children's Dentistry. It's an entertaining and escapist experience: the waiting room and front desk look like any nicely furnished medical office, but the whole treatment area is fitted out like a jungle, with a giant tree in the center, carved "stone" faces on pillars, and painted backdrops in the spaces where the dentistry takes place. (The fanciful installation was created by Larson Construction, known for its work at zoos and theme parks.) Kids who are waiting can watch DVDs or play video games while sitting on carved "boulders." A host of jungle-theme stuffed animals and artwork fills every corner of the space. At the end of their visits children earn a token to spend in the prize machine. This dental practice is thriving by combining a unique physical space with great service and superior patient care.[10] Dr. Culp took an experience that was dry and even scary and created an environment that helps draws patients in.

Meaningful and authentic

The idea that an experience should be meaningful shows up frequently in retail research. Branding expert Marc Gobé believes that products and companies should appeal to consumer's emotions, and he passionately argues that companies must prove their worth and good citizenship for continued success. Leslie Wexner, CEO of the Limited, Inc., helped build the Wexner Center for the Arts at Ohio State University in Columbus. The cultural center benefits the city of Columbus as well as the Limited employees headquartered there and reflects prestigiously on Wexner's company.[11] The Body Shop and Aveda have built their successes both on quality products harvested from the earth and their reputations for giving back to local communities.

In search of the authentic. Authors David Lewis and Darren Bridger believe that today's consumers crave authentic experiences and products and want to see a "meaningful, emotional, intellectual, or practical reward."[12] Authentic experiences are based on real, rather than fabricated, environments or artifacts. You can intentionally create an authentic experience. At the Crickethead Inn Bed & Breakfast in Tucson, Arizona, owner Michael Lord has nestled a concrete watering hole a few yards from the back porch. All kinds of wild animals—from bobcats to javelinas—drink there, providing a magical experience for guests.

People believe that "real things" are powerful.[13] What do we believe is authentic? As life becomes more mass-produced, handmade objects and old objects, which carry meaning over time, become rarer and more highly valued.[14]

Quintessence. Researchers describe quintessential things as having a "rare and mysterious capacity to be just exactly what they ought to be." Quintessence is something that feels magically desirable, is achieved over a long period of time, and comes from people's attitudes toward a quality product, not from a marketing campaign. Some examples of quintessential products are the Swiss Army knife, the Zippo lighter, the Wham-O Frisbee, and Coca-Cola.[15] Sometimes tourists will not buy objects that don't match their perception of what authentic should be. In Papua New Guinea hand-carved "storyboards" don't sell if the scenes are painted with bright colors or include people listening to the radio or riding in a motorboat.[16]

In Istanbul several old houses near the main tourist attractions have been converted into small hotels. Painted traditional pastel colors, they are furnished with Turkish antiques to represent nineteenth-century middle-class homes. Full of divans, Turkish carpets, crocheted covers, and swagged curtains, they feel authentic to travelers.[17]

When you are what you say you are. Authors Joseph Pine and James Gilmore define authenticity in business as being true to self. Authentic businesses are perceived as true in who they are, what they offer, and why they exist. Pine and Gilmore also observe that an authentic business describes itself to customers in a way that matches its true nature.[18] Marketing guru Seth Godin believes that marketers must create authentic stories in order to succeed in today's low-trust world.[19] This craving for authenticity is an ace in the hole for museums; we have the real "stuff" that our potential visitors crave. Tap into this trend with your museum's marketing, programs, and exhibitions.

Restoration Hardware, an upscale, retro home-furnishings chain in the U.S., has been successful by tapping into people's yearning for authentic times past. This yearning reflects the genuine passion of founder Stephen Gordon, who has stocked the stores with things he himself values, like the original 1955 Duncan yo-yo. Restoration Hardware features products people remember from childhood, ingenious toys, and high-quality furniture and fixtures that offer both emotional and practical rewards.[20] While Restoration Hardware offers

Authentic businesses are perceived as true in who they are, what they offer, and why they exist.

fabricated nostalgia, some museums are taking their authentic artifacts and creating immersion environments that bring the objects to life while tapping into people's nostalgia. One of the best examples I've seen was an exhibition called *Chicago Goes to War* at the Chicago History Museum. It offered walk-through vignettes of 1940s Chicago created using artifacts from the collection, with drawers that opened to reveal things like letters sent home by soldiers during World War II.

Creating a "third place"

Professor Ray Oldenburg believes that service businesses play a crucial role in a healthy society. He calls it being the "third place." (Home is the first place and work the second.)[21] There are few suburban neighborhoods in the U.S. where you can easily find third places, but in Europe they are everywhere: the English corner pub, the French café, and the German beer garden. Third places are centrally located, usually within walking distance from home or work; the "entertainment" is created by the presence and conversation of the regulars. Third places provide novelty, a healthy perspective on life, a spiritual tonic, and easy socializing with a set of casual friends. Third places also take the burden off personal relationships by giving people a break from their families. The success of Borders Books and Starbucks attests to the need for third places in America. How can you encourage dropping in and hanging out at your site?[22] Can you build a following of "regulars?" Create a community? Introduce your visitors to each other and provide opportunities for conversation? According to Oldenburg, steady business and profits will follow.

The Yahoo! Link@Sheraton is turning hotel lobbies into third places. Besides refreshments, WiFi, workstations, and plasma televisions, they also furnish visitors with a virtual concierge service—information on local weather and restaurants, and travel directions. Sheraton understands that hotel guests want the choice of congregating rather than just staying in their rooms.[23] Shopping malls are following this trend by creating family lounges and "comfort zones" where shoppers can rest.[24] Reinier Evers of trendwatching.com calls third places "Being Spaces."[25] These contemporary multi-use public spaces offer free WiFi access, ports for plugging in and recharging cell phones, leather seating, coffee, copiers and fax machines, and other amenities. Can your site offer this kind of multi-use space and provide a valuable service in your visitors' lives, or draw in nearby hotel guests with these types of services?

Offering multiple rewards at your site

Catering to the learner-gatherer culture. As you think through the kinds of experiences you're offering your visitors, consider how you can add elements to round out your experience while remaining true to your mission. The exercises on page 159 will help you apply these concepts to your site. The good news, both from consumer studies and from museum researchers John Falk and Lynn Dierking, is that people enjoy learning. Learning something is often a reward in itself.[26] People also enjoy being social with a group, so design your site to allow them to gather and interact. Provide them with a challenge, make them feel comfortable, help them learn and participate.

The Grove in San Diego has tapped into the knitting trend. This shop sells books and home furnishings, but its most notable feature is a group of knitters usually found sitting around the table in the back. By cultivating skilled knitters the Grove is creating a market for the beautiful yarn they stock. The store offers all six leisure-time rewards. Their customers enjoy social interaction, active participation, and the challenge of learning new and worthwhile things, all in a comfortable setting. As you build upon your existing experience, consider how *you* can create a self-sustaining flow of visitors who'll support you into the future. Offering a well-rounded experience—entertaining, relaxing, *and* educational—is key to satisfying visitors and getting them to come back, which we'll talk about in the next chapter.

CHAPTER 4

Getting them to come back

It's safe to say that if you have visitors, you want them to come to your site regularly. If you haven't consciously decided how often you want your visitors to return, this chapter will help you define your hopes and expectations as clear goals. Having goals allows you to use your resources wisely and sharpens the focus of your efforts for the best results.

"Getting them to come back" can be broken down into two parts. "Getting them" is your goal. "To come back" is the behavior you are trying to influence. Influencing visitors' behavior is tricky for many reasons, as I'll explain throughout this chapter. I'm going to cover two broad areas of research into the psychology of behavior change. I've named these areas self-help and persuasion.[1] First I'll give you some background on each, then we'll see how each can be applied to your site and your visitors.

Next, to make the idea of behavior change as concrete as possible, we'll look at four aspects of visitor behavior that you might want to influence: frequency, duration, engagement, and off-site actions. The exercises on pages 161–62 will help you set specific goals for changing the behavior of your visitors.

The challenge of changing people's behavior

Self-help and persuasion

The study of human behavior is incredibly complex, and a thorough examination of it is far beyond the scope of this book. But because I believe the information is critical to your success, I am presenting the essence of this research as two useful categories for us to discuss. In the self-help realm, researchers of behavior change see certain human behaviors—such as addictions—as negative. These researchers study people who successfully change their behaviors, looking for patterns that might help others change themselves. This research is usually applied to help people change negative personal behaviors—like successfully quitting an addiction or losing weight. We'll explore how it applies to informal learning sites. Sites whose missions support a visitor's personal goals regarding fitness, wellness, or care of the environment are the ones that can best use the six stages for behavior change explored below.

Other researchers study persuasion—how people can be influenced. Their work doesn't view persuasion as good or bad. They study which techniques are effective and try to determine why. This type of research is applied extensively in advertising and marketing. Informal learning sites already use persuasion techniques; I'll show you how to apply them beyond advertising and marketing.

Self-help

There are thousands of self-help books available, but I'm going to focus on one that has a particularly useful framework. James Prochaska, John Norcross, and Carlo DiClemente studied hundreds of people who successfully quit bad habits by permanently changing their lifestyles. Their book, *Changing for Good*, identifies six stages a person goes through to successfully change a habit.[2] Not only did the authors clearly identify and define these stages for the first time, they found specific ways to help people move themselves from one stage to the next. I'll briefly summarize their work here, as it might apply to visitors working on weight-loss, fitness, or other personal goals.

- **Pre-contemplation.** People in pre-contemplation (stage 1) don't want to admit they have a problem. They just want everyone to stop bugging them! They are resistant to change. In fact, they're convinced that trying to change would be futile. One of the self-help exercises in *Changing for Good* is to make a list of the positives and negatives related to changing. In order to progress from pre-contemplation to the next stage, a person needs to be able to *double* the number of positive benefits on his list. So, if someone listed six benefits of quitting smoking, he'd need to find six more benefits he believes in before he is ready to move to the next stage.

You may have visitors who are pre-contemplators. They're the ones who come to your zoo or aquarium on a tour that's part of a convention and couldn't care less about your environmental mission. The most effective way to communicate with this audience is to spell out the benefits of a specific environmental behavior, like lowering their electric bills by switching to compact fluorescent light bulbs. Or, maybe some of your members received a membership as a gift but have never used it. Sending a letter listing the benefits of becoming an active visitor could help nudge them along.

- **Contemplation.** *Changing for Good* says that people who are struggling to understand their problem are in the contemplation stage (stage 2). They need to talk and get information. They're not yet ready to prepare for action because they are afraid of failing and wary of change. If you are an outdoor site like a park, arboretum, or garden, you could offer contemplators classes or support groups for planning how to start an exercise program (before they actually start exercising), or to live a more earth-friendly lifestyle. In order to move to the next stage, a contemplator must be able to take the list of negatives he made in stage 1 and cut it in half. So, if he started with ten negatives, he must be willing to cross five of them off his list. When he can do that, he's ready for the preparation stage.

- **Preparation.** People at this stage (3) will take action within a month. It's important for them to announce their intentions to their friends, families, or colleagues and to create a detailed six-month plan for action, including techniques they'll use to prevent relapses. An effective strategy for them is to list the benefits of changing and review the list often.

  A visitor in the preparation stage needs a framework for making positive changes. Think of offering him such things as detailed shopping lists for restocking his house with earth-friendly items, books targeted to this stage, or exercise clothing for the class he will begin within a month. You might also help him track his progress by sending him weekly e-mails offering encouragement and tips on relapse prevention.

- **Action.** People in action (stage 4) are busy practicing healthy behaviors, like exercising, recycling, or reducing their carbon footprint. This stage is the one most commonly focused on, but the authors of

Changing for Good found that it is no more or less important than the other stages. It does take the greatest commitment of time and energy. Since the action stage is the longest and busiest, it affords you many opportunities to serve a visitor—to help him focus on positive outcomes and reinforce what he needs to do to stay in the action stage for at least six months. You might provide him with monthly coupons to reward himself or check in with him to see what else he might need. People in the action stage can use pocket guides to restaurants and grocery stores (like the Seafood Watch card produced by the Monterey Bay Aquarium). Consider sending e-mail announcements each month to help keep people motivated. You can also create an online community to allow people to encourage each other. When they've been in action for six months, then and only then are they ready for maintenance. (In fact, if they move to that stage too quickly, they tend to relapse.)

- **Maintenance.** When they're entering maintenance (stage 5), visitors need help staying committed and preparing themselves to face new stresses or crises. The maintenance stage can last for years, as people learn to make consistent lifestyle choices. You can help support visitors in the maintenance stage by providing classes or handouts during known times of stress—during vacation season and around the holidays—or if you know they have gone through a job change, marriage, divorce, or the loss of a family member.

- **Termination.** This final stage is not relevant to our discussion. It applies to certain behaviors like smoking, when wanting to smoke eventually stops. Other behaviors—like adopting an earth-friendly lifestyle—require lifelong maintenance.

If your museum, zoo, park, garden, arboretum, or aquarium deals with conservation issues, I recommend you read *Changing for Good* to learn about the six stages in detail. You'll see more clearly how you can identify the stage a visitor is in. Then you'll be better able to support his efforts to change by creating classes and other products and services tailored to his needs at each stage. Some art museums are beginning to offer yoga or tai chi classes in their gallery spaces, so many types of sites can apply this information.

Persuasion

Retailers, marketers, and advertisers have long studied and tried to influence consumers' behavior. Their field, consumer psychology, has been around for decades. Researchers study why people buy certain brands, what makes advertising effective, and how music, color, and images affect our buying behavior. It's undoubtedly the best-funded research of its type, since there are vast amounts of money to be made from the knowledge that the research supports.

Robert Webb has taken research done in the consumer field and applied it to museums. He believes that human behavior is consistent regardless of whether you're in a store or a museum—and that the wealth of consumer studies available can benefit museums and similar facilities.[3] For example, Webb's findings could be applied to a text label on a mummy in a museum. The label must attract a visitor's attention *and* hold it long enough for him to read and understand the text. It's the same attention-getting process used for ads in a magazine or cereal boxes on the shelf of a grocery store. You may have heard about attracting and holding power if you've read museum visitor studies. I'll talk about specific methods of effective communication in Chapter 11.

Retail anthropologist Paco Underhill has been studying people's behavior in stores, malls, and banks for more than two decades.[4] His highly entertaining book *Why We Buy* describes many behaviors in the retail arena that also apply to the nonprofit world: how "packages" are designed, where elements like exhibits or signs are placed, and whether people feel comfortable and well oriented within a space. I'll discuss Underhill's findings throughout Section 3: Your Site.

Putting persuasion to work for you

- **Imagine that.** Researchers have found that engaging people's imaginations is a powerful tool for changing their behavior. If you can get them to imagine taking your class, or using a product from your store, they are more likely to buy or use it.

- **Repeat (and repeat) your message.** Repetition creates preferences. That's why those "Buy 10, Get 1 Free" cards are effective.[5] The visitor is motivated by the freebie to make ten purchases, visiting your site ten times. In the process you become part of that person's routine.

- **Up front and personal.** If you are creating flyers, include a map with your site's location circled and your hours listed in a place that's easy to see. Making the information practical and personally relevant makes people more likely to visit.[6]
- **Here's looking at you.** If you want to get people to follow rules at your site, try putting an image of human eyes at the top of the poster or sign. Researchers have found that people are more likely to cooperate when they have a subtle feeling they're being watched.[7]

Aspect of visitor behavior #1: Frequency

Now we'll apply this research to your site. We're going to look at four aspects of your visitors' behavior. The first, frequency, focuses on how often someone visits your site. Think about your organization for a minute. Is there an ideal frequency for you? Be realistic, but also dream big. If a family has a membership to your site, they can make an unlimited number of visits for the price of that annual membership, so you might not have considered whether it matters how often they visit. In their new book, *Thriving in the Knowledge Age*, John Falk and Beverly Sheppard suggest that museums could charge people more who visit more often, while adding customized services to create higher value for these visitors.[8]

Consider the lifetime value of a visitor. If someone spends $75 a year for a membership, purchases $25 worth of merchandise in your store during each visit, and comes in four times a year, that visitor is worth at least $1,750 to you over ten years.[9] If you could double the number of times each member visited—and the spending level stayed the same— you could nearly double your revenue stream without having to attract any new visitors!

Frequency is a key to financial health. It measures how much you are part of your visitors' lifestyles. "Lifestyle visitors" are incredibly loyal, helping to spread your message to others. According to a recent study, forty-seven percent of frequent visitors to cultural organizations are also donors.[10]

To develop frequency, keep in mind that the experience you offer should be both consistently good and constantly fresh. Do you offer enough variety in your experience to get people to visit once a

An aquarium decides it would like every member to visit once a month. But research shows that, on average, their members visit twice a year. The aquarium has a lot of work to do to improve the frequency. They set this measurable objective: to develop a new hands-on program that changes every month. Each member is mailed an annual "Passport to Ocean Treasures" with spaces for twelve stamps. Visitors are rewarded at the end of the year for four, eight, or twelve visits stamped on their completed "passports." The rewards are gift certificates of increasing value to spend in the on-site store or on future programs.

month? Once a quarter? Have you thought of installing a revolving display—the "favorite object of the month"—just inside the entrance to your site? You might have a variety of staff members—not just curators—create the interpretive texts. How about asking the manager of the museum store, the custodian, the security guard, the head of membership to write label copy? Not only would that get more of your staff involved in your collection (which has a ripple effect on their families), but you'd also be providing fresh points of view for your visitors. Or you could invite local schools or artists to interpret pieces from your collection on a rotating basis. There are many ways that setting frequency goals can help you fulfill your community mission.

Aspect of visitor behavior #2: Duration

Duration refers to the length of time you want visitors to spend at your site. It might be ninety minutes for a class, an hour for a meal, or two hours for your new exhibition. How long is your "ideal" visit? Do you want to extend it? Research at malls shows that adding a food court increases the length of people's visits by more than an hour.[11] And, if people extend their "stay time" from one to two hours, they will double their spending.[12]

At nonprofits duration is an important measure of how deeply visitors have engaged in your offerings. Longer stays mean that people are soaking up your content. If your site is fairly remote and attendance is not as high as you'd like, think about how long it takes people to travel to you and tailor your services accordingly. How long is it realistic to expect their visits to be, if you add in total travel time? What supplementary services could you provide to round out visitors' experiences and make it worth their while to visit you? Some of these services will produce revenue.[13] If travel time is more than two hours, offer food service or a picnic area with food for sale. Consider advertising a full package of offerings, so that people can picture themselves making a day of it with you.

A museum store might decide that the perfect visit is thirty minutes, but visitors are only spending fifteen. Even worse, only three out of ten visitors buy anything, meaning the conversion rate (buyers divided by browsers) is only thirty-three percent. The manager decides to offer demonstrations at the beginning of each hour, allowing shoppers to try out various products, educational CDs, or toys. The store's existing software system tracks whether sales increase on the demonstration days.

Aspect of visitor behavior #3: Engagement

What you want visitors to do while they're at your site is engage. This means that they read labels, manipulate interactive displays, take photographs, talk to members of your staff,[14] and play together. All those behaviors increase learning.[15] Engagement can also be measured through the attracting and holding power of exhibits or signs. If you have a retail store, you want visitors to take a shopping basket, talk to a salesperson, touch the merchandise, and try on clothing. All those behaviors foster a feeling of connection and increase sales.[16]

You can create engagement by making your content personally relevant and by following the guidelines for communication outlined in Chapter 11, as well as by making sure that much of what you exhibit and sell engages all five senses, as discussed in Chapter 12.

Aspect of visitor behavior #4:
Off-site actions

The fourth and final aspect of visitor behavior is off-site actions. What do you want visitors to do after they leave? The first is to tell friends about your site. The best advertising you can ever get is positive word of mouth, because it's coming from a trusted source rather than from the producer of the experience. Think about ways you can reward your visitors for telling friends about you, perhaps with a discount or freebie.[17]

Second, you might want them to take part in fundraising or political advocacy, or to volunteer for a cause related to your mission. One of my regular haunts in San Diego, the South Bark Dog Wash, is community oriented and promotes the causes of pet adoption, spaying, and neutering. They also encourage customers to support animal rights by serving as a local information center on lost dogs and pet-rescue efforts during disasters like Hurricane Katrina.

For museums and other nonprofits, there may be many goals related to off-site behavior. For conservation-related organizations like zoos, aquariums, parks, and nature centers, consumer psychology has developed an offshoot called conservation psychology.[18] Conservation psychology blends self-help techniques (like the six stages outlined in *Changing for Good*) with persuasion. Nature-based sites might actively encourage visitors to recycle, drive fuel-efficient vehicles, and choose sustainably harvested fish in order to save animal habitats.[19]

A state park decides it would like more visitors to carpool. This would cut down on crowding in the parking lot, save gasoline, and reduce greenhouse-gas emissions, all of which support the site's conservation mission. The park begins offering a coupon to local residents, advertising the carpooling program with a reduced entry fee.

Now it's time to put behavior change to work for you. Use the exercises on pages 161–62 to set your own goals for changing your visitors' behavior. Defining exactly what you hope to achieve, and how often, will help you focus your efforts, however you define success. In the next chapter we'll examine how to build a strong brand for your site—one that will help draw visitors steadily over time.

> The best advertising you can ever get is positive word of mouth, because it's coming from a trusted source rather than from the producer of the experience.

From loyalty to lifestyle: The South Bark Dog Wash

You want to create loyalty in your visitors so that you become part of their lifestyles. How do you go from loyalty to lifestyle? I started going to the South Bark Dog Wash with our golden retriever puppy, Buddy. This self-service pet grooming and retail store is conveniently located near our favorite off-leash dog park, so Buddy could get happily slobbery-muddy and then come home clean and soft after a bath. We soon made it a monthly habit, as the staff members were friendly, fun, and informative. When Buddy was young, we took our first puppy-training class there, and we ended up taking three more classes over the years. Then we began buying our food, flea treatments, squeaky balls, and rawhide chewies from South Bark. When Buddy needed a new collar and leash for Christmas, guess where we bought them?

We go every four weeks, spending about an hour and buying far more than the basic $8 bath. We enjoy the "Buy 6, Get 1 Free" wash cards, as owner Donna Walker rings the bell loudly whenever we get a free wash. She's great at giving random and unexpected discounts, like a free blow dry. The store keeps track of our kibble and treat purchases; after every tenth bag we get one of those free, too.

South Bark's goal is to serve visitors for the life spans of their pets. For a dog that lives ten years, that could easily mean $10,000 in sales. The owners don't try to oversell us, but they've created such a fun and compelling experience that we gladly shop there. Going to South Bark is part of our lifestyle, because it's a pleasurable, well-rounded, consistent experience. While it is for-profit, it combines interactive services, education, and advocacy in a beautiful model that works for nonprofit sites as well.

CHAPTER 5

What's in a name? Defining your brand

Every business, including your site, has a brand image. The state park with the beat-up wayside signs, the slick new science center, the historic-house museum—they all convey a brand image, whether their board members or managers have thought about it or not.

Every aspect of your operation—your name, logo, and location; the condition of your facilities; your Web site, printed materials, voice-mail message, and staff—sends a message about your brand.[1] If you have designed a strong identity for your site, consistent with your goals and long-range plans, then your brand is probably doing its job. But if you are just starting out, struggling to maintain attendance, or not making enough revenue, then looking at your business through the branding lens can be helpful.

Many sites design a logo and print business cards or a letterhead, but haven't had time to consider their brand image as a whole. The tools in this chapter will help you define your brand clearly so that you can coordinate *all* the elements into one seamless impression. The same branding techniques that help multibillion-dollar companies sell soda or jeans can set your site apart from your leisure-time competition, while signaling your true nonprofit mission.

A crash course in branding

Branding—burning a symbol into skin—has been used for thousands of years to show ownership. In the last hundred years the word has evolved from meaning "I own this" to "You want to own this."[2]

Modern branding grew out of the world of advertising, which first appeared when factories started mass producing consumer goods. When there was only one general store in town, selling just one kind of flour in a large bin, there was no need for advertising. (When there was only one museum in town, offering its unique educational experience, it didn't need to advertise, either.)

You tell your story. They buy your brand. Modern branding is much broader than simply a name or a logo. To be considered a true brand today, the company or product must provide both functional and emotional benefits to the customer.[4] It's similar to my definition of the visitor experience as taking place both inside and outside; a true brand exists in the minds of your visitors, created by concrete actions you take. It is their perception of your site.[5]

Early advertising was simple; it introduced you to a product and its virtues.[3] As similar products from different manufacturers became available, advertising became more sophisticated. Name brands started to appear whenever consumers had many identical choices. Early name brands like Aunt Jemima and Quaker Oats were based on friendly faces, mirroring kindly local shopkeepers'.

Modern branding is, in part, telling a story about a product to convince customers to buy it, instead of buying another (nearly identical) product. An adman from the 1950s, Rosser Reeves, described branding as creating a "unique selling proposition" for a product. He would take two quarters from his pocket and tell clients that his job was to make customers believe that one quarter was worth more than the other.[6] The customer is buying the story. For them the Ivory Soap story is more appealing than the Irish Spring story, even though both soaps smell nice and will get the consumer clean.

The successful public television program *Antiques Roadshow* illustrates how stories create value in an object. When the owner of an antique knows the story behind it (its "provenance" in museum lingo), the value of the object can rise dramatically. A chair from the 1750s in good condition can be valuable. If the chair belonged to Thomas Jefferson, it's worth much more. If the founding father sat in the chair while signing the Declaration of Independence, the value of the chair skyrockets.

When your brand really *is* different. Today, branding experts say that Reeves's statement is only partly true. Branding can also be used to clarify and own differences that truly do exist. This is important, because if a company doesn't successfully brand a new product or service, another company can copy it, do a better job of branding it, and then "own" that innovation in the marketplace.[7]

A brand is a promise

Beyond being merely a story about a product, a brand is a promise to customers about what they can expect from a business.[8] It should be "consistent, intentional, differentiated, and valuable."[9] Ronseal, a paint and varnish company in the UK, has this brand promise: "It does exactly what it says on the tin."[10] A business in Virginia called the History Factory helps companies harness the power of their corporate stories, promising to "Unlock the Power of the Past."[11]

A brand promise should also capture people's imaginations.[12] A television ad campaign in 2005–6 for the Nissan Pathfinder promised that an owner would "tell better stories." The ads showed a Pathfinder driver relating an involved adventure story—made possible by the car—when he was asked how he spent his weekend. The Pathfinder brochure ends with the line "Let the storytelling begin."[13]

Branding is the worst thing that ever happened to us

A number of authors tell you that branding is ruining our world, invading our cultural institutions, and manipulating us every minute of every day. At its worst, branding creates value out of nothing, putting a high price tag on a cheap item while taking advantage of the consumer, the low-paid sweatshop worker, and the underpaid sales clerk.[14] Critiques of branding can sound bitter about the huge financial gains of global brands, as if the companies are selling the modern-day equivalent of the emperor's new clothes. Whether it's the Marlboro Man, Disney, or Tommy Hilfiger, brands are powerful entities that influence people's lives in a way that was unthinkable thirty years ago. For this reason many museum people are mistrustful of branding—and sometimes of the marketing manager who is promoting it.

How well-respected workers affect your brand. If your site sells products that are manufactured overseas, be aware that a growing number of consumers want to know who is making the products they buy and how those people are treated. Be sure anything you carry in your shop is produced according to standards that support your mission, and let your visitors know your policy regarding this issue.

Regardless of where you buy your merchandise, the way you treat your employees is another key element in your success. One of the biggest criticisms of companies like Wal-Mart and McDonald's is that they build their success on the backs of employees. They don't pay well, and they often deliberately structure job schedules to avoid paying benefits. The Merriam-Webster Dictionary now defines "McJob" as a low-paying one, requiring little skill and offering little opportunity for advancement.[15] This hiring practice may work in the short term, but in the long run it's an unwise financial strategy. Some museum employees have attempted to unionize to protect themselves from exploitation, and employee associations with the power to challenge management are now common at larger institutions. The best organizations—whether for profit or not—the ones with long-term growth and strong brands, are also ones that treat their employees well.[16] We'll talk more about this "people first" approach in Chapter 6.

Avoid logo overload. Another criticism of branding is that logos seem to be on every surface, even the bathroom walls.[17] Author James Twitchell calls it "logorrhea."[18] Sites must be sensitive to consumer overload—when branding is everywhere and there seems to be no escape. School curriculum materials may now include brand names as part of a sponsorship deal, which many parents and educators feel is going too far. But cash-strapped school systems are desperately looking for ways to keep books and computers in their classrooms and their gyms supplied with sports equipment.[19] So the choice is not an easy one, and often educators feel that they are making a deal with the devil in order to provide needed services for students. Your site may be involved in curriculum development, so set a policy up front for dealing with this issue.

Branding is the best thing that ever happened to us

On the flip side is the promise of branding—the power of stories. The most passionate voice for the power of positive branding is Marc Gobé. His firm, d/g*, has worked on brands like Godiva chocolates, Victoria's Secret, and Coca-Cola. Over the years Gobé has come to believe that brands have a civic responsibility to serve the public, better people's lives, and be authentic, not manipulative. His second book, *Citizen Brand*, is a call to action for companies to be honest, trustworthy, and create a dialogue with their customers. Gobé's book is worthwhile for nonprofit staff members to read, as it helps explain what companies may be seeking when they form partnerships with cultural institutions.

The generous giants. Corporate brands can do a lot of good if they are directed to do so. They provide financial support, goods, and services to cultural and educational organizations and can effect positive changes in the environment through sustainable manufacturing practices.[20] Conservation International is now working with McDonald's, Starbucks, and Office Depot to help these companies implement better environmental practices among their global suppliers.[21] Wal-Mart has just announced a broader "green policy" that includes offering a line of organic products, which environmentalists hope will have a positive effect on Wal-Mart's global supply chain.[22]

Rebranding as rejuvenation. Many cultural organizations, including California State Parks,[23] New York's Guggenheim Museum,[24] and London's Tate galleries[25] have gone through a formal rebranding process. I was impressed with the rebranding campaign undertaken by the Atlanta Botanical Garden. Through a board member, this site was able to get $250,000 in branding services donated. Their ambitious goal was to increase attendance by twenty percent a year for five years. A consumer research study, undertaken as part of the rebranding process, found that the garden had a great reputation but wasn't really considered a destination. The new campaign was designed to help potential customers see the garden as a "lifestyle brand, a rejuvenating oasis." It worked. The number of paying visitors increased by 25% in the first year after rebranding, and there was an astounding 130% increase in attendance for May 2004 (compared to the previous May) for the garden's exhibition of Dale Chihuly's works in glass.[26]

The Washington State History Museum recently completed a successful rebranding campaign with the tag line "These Walls Can Talk." Admissions and donations are on the rise, and the experience has had a positive effect on staff morale as well.[27]

So, is branding the worst or the best thing in our culture? Like any powerful tool used with skill, it can be either. Branding is happening all around us, and there is no likelihood it will be going away any time soon. Your strongest competitors are using this tool for their benefit, and might be burning you with it. Branding your site is a way to enter their arena and make your institution stronger and more successful.

Your target visitors

A great description of how to use branding comes from Marc Gobé. In the late 1980s, his firm was hired to create the brand identity for a new chain of stores called Express being developed by the Limited, Inc. While struggling with the project, Gobé became inspired by Princess Stephanie of Monaco and imagined designing the store to appeal to her. He developed storyboards showing pictures of her, her house, her clothes, and her hangouts. He created what he called an "aspirational customer" for Express, one for whom the store—and Princess Stephanie's persona—would have unmistakable appeal. The buyers used his ideas to purchase products, and the stores' interiors were designed around the concept.[28]

There is debate about whether there's such a thing as an ideal, "aspirational" visitor. The notion can sound elitist to staff at nonprofits. But, no matter how broad your mission, it is unlikely that your site appeals to everyone in the world. Your target markets might be relatively narrow, or fairly broad. Deciding which visitors you are trying to reach can be a key tool in helping you focus your efforts. You can always expand the concept of a single target visitor to include several groups if that is appropriate to your site and mission. It's better to do a great job of meeting the needs of your target visitors than to do a mediocre job of serving "everyone."

Jon Schallert, a marketing consultant who works with small businesses to turn them into consumer destinations, was helping a podiatrist define her "perfect customer." First the podiatrist said her target customers were female, but that wasn't specific enough for Schallert. Then she said she wanted to attract "females forty to eighty years old who have foot problems." Schallert told the doctor to get even more specific, and her target audience became "women who are basically healthy, have the money to take care of themselves, and need me to help them maintain their active lifestyle of golfing, running, hiking, kayaking, and bicycling." With that, they both knew she had defined her ideal customer base.[29]

Market segmentation is another way of identifying your audience. This technique homes in on groups that share important characteristics relating to your site. These characteristics include attitudes about your brand, values certain people hold, and behaviors they embrace. Shedd Aquarium in Chicago has used this tool to better understand who is *not* attending its site and why.[30] The site has identified five key market segments that they've dubbed Enrichment Seekers, Edutainment Enthusiasts, Fun-Loving Suburbanites, Young Urban Explorers, and Idle Empty Nesters.[31] The Shedd has used these five targeted groups to help them develop ad campaigns, plan special exhibitions, add new member services, and drive their master planning process.

What makes people visit? Taking a more psychological approach, John Falk and his colleagues at the Institute for Learning Innovation (ILI) have been studying how "situated identity" influences visitors' learning and behavior. They have identified five motivation types that embody the main reasons people visit a site. They've named the types Explorer, Professional/Hobbyist, Experience Seeker, Spiritual Pilgrim, and Facilitator. Recent research at ILI using this framework showed that identity-related motivations directly influenced how visitors used a zoo or aquarium as well as what they learned and remembered. Similar results are emerging from research conducted at science centers, history museums, and botanical gardens.[32]

The value of a name

As part of your branding process, take a look at your name. Does it state clearly what your site is about? Does it instantly tell people whether you are fun or serious, educational, escapist, or entertaining? If not, you may want to change it.

Deciding on a name change can be a long and complex process, especially if there are donors or sponsors to be considered. Despite these challenges, some sites have crafted new names that make them more appealing to their target audience. The Strybing Arboretum and Botanical Gardens in San Francisco's Golden Gate Park went through a branding process. Their old name did not help draw visitors or aptly describe who they were. ("Strybing" is a donor's name—hard to pronounce and meaningless to visitors. In addition, "arboretum," a Latin term for tree preserve, may be unfamiliar to visitors.) The site is now San Francisco

Botanical Garden at Strybing Arboretum (with the last three words in smaller type). The garden's new logo de-emphasizes the old name without dropping it altogether.[33] The Chicago Historical Society became the Chicago History Museum, after market testing showed that both "historical" and "society" had negative or elitist connotations for visitors.

Use the power of branding to create an engaging story about your site, one that appeals to potential visitors and demonstrates the benefits you offer them. The exercises on pages 164–65 will help you begin to put branding to work for you. Defining your business personality and developing target-visitor profiles create unity in your presentation to visitors, letting them know that you are there for *them*. It also helps you spend your marketing and advertising dollars effectively. In the next chapter we'll look at your employees. Empowered employees have the biggest influence on your visitor experience; everyone who works for you—employees and volunteers alike—reflects your brand.

CHAPTER 6

Putting people first

Bali, the experience. My husband and I arrived in Bali late in the evening and got through customs. Our driver from the Villas Hotel and Spa was waiting for us with the warmest, most beautiful smile we'd ever seen. As we drove through the dark to the town of Seminyak, a riot of sensory impressions flashed past. The driver swung a hard left off the main road down an unpaved alley, and we were suddenly there, at the entrance to the Villas. Thatched-roof palapas, a fountain, lovely cushions on a teak bench, and more smiles greeted us as we stepped into the balmy night air. We were checked in promptly and welcomed, and a staff member explained the accommodations. A key on a hand-carved ring opened the gate at no. 21, our home for the next week. While we were being shown the amenities, we drank in the sculptures, the pool, the garden, and the shaded kitchen. The staff member showed us how to work the air conditioner in the bedroom and pointed out the menu for breakfast and room service and the basket for laundry. Everywhere we looked were small arrangements of cut flowers—in a circle around the soap dish, on the dining table, on the pillows. (You see these meticulous flower arrangements anywhere you go in Bali; I even saw one decorating a toilet-paper holder in a restaurant bathroom.)

Smiles make an impression. While staying at the Villas was a once-in-a-lifetime experience, what stands out for both of us is the people we met. Everyone seemed to have a beautiful smile, with an inner light that shone through. Every morning our breakfast order was served in our kitchen with radiant smiles. The grounds crew came in to tend the garden, seeming truly happy with their jobs. The drivers we hired to take us around were amazing, explaining why the cars were decorated with small star-shaped baskets (it was a "metal gods" holiday), telling us about the seasonal kite festival, and shedding light on many other things we didn't understand. The people at the spa were truly caring. While I was basking in affordable luxury, my feet soaking in flower-petal water, I marveled at the beauty of the place and the people who made it so memorable. Is every hotel in Bali like the Villas? I have no idea. Bali is quite beautiful, but the Villas is very special, because the people who work there make it so. We would go back to the Villas in a heartbeat, knowing our experience would again be lovely, filled with Balinese smiles, food, flowers, and comfort.

The experience *is* the people

Human interaction is the key component of the visitor experience. It's your brand come to life. Here's how crucial it is, according to a senior marketing executive. "I can do everything right in marketing—have the right messages, target the right customer, make the right promises—but it is all for naught if the $7-an-hour person at the cash register is having a bad day. That is the last impression of my brand the customer will have."[1] Every person who interacts with your visitor has an enormous impact on his or her experience. Whether they are employees or volunteers, your security guards, cashiers, receptionists, librarians, docents, educators, curators, rangers, gardeners, and custodians are essential to your visitor's experience. Here are some guidelines for doing it right.

Passion and a positive attitude are free. As we found at the Villas, a warm greeting and a smile are critical. Visitors should know that you are genuinely glad they have arrived. Betsy Sanders, a top customer-service trainer for the department store Nordstrom, believes customer service boils down to two things: "To serve and to be kind." The way to achieve what she calls "fabled customer service" is to meet all expectations, then exceed them.[2] The customer service stories that result become legends: Nordstrom will accept any merchandise back for exchange or refund. When they bought out several stores, they found themselves facing a customer who was unhappy with some snow chains purchased before the store changed hands. Even though Nordstrom *no longer sold snow chains*, they refunded the customer's money.[3] Do your training and policies empower your employees to offer that level of response to a visitor's complaint?

Lexus Motors has made its mark in the competitive U.S. auto industry with its mission of treating customers as "guests in our own home." A Lexus customer in Texas was driving his pregnant wife to the hospital for her delivery when he realized they wouldn't make it in time. He headed instead to his Lexus dealership, since they'd "always been great to deal with." The customer's daughter, Isabella Alexus, was born on the front seat of the SUV with the help of Lexus staff.[4] When I think about the typical impression we have of car salesmen, that story astounds me. Would any of your visitors choose you to help them in a moment of such great personal significance?

Customer service is inborn

One theme emerges when we hear about exceptional companies. Nordstrom hires for the smile and attitude, preferring people with no prior retail experience.[5] Southwest Airlines hires for attitude and trains for skills.[6] Perhaps business consultants Kevin and Jackie Freiberg say it best: "Avoid people who suck."[7] Exceptional companies look for a positive attitude and screen for passion. Disney recommends avoiding pessimists.[8] In fact, part of Disney's core ideology is "no cynicism."[9] No amount of customer-service training can turn someone who doesn't want to work with visitors into someone who enjoys it.

How do you screen for passion? Planet Honda in Union, New Jersey, is one of the most successful Honda dealerships in the U.S. They ask these questions when they interview: "What is your purpose in life?" "What do you want to accomplish in the next twenty-four months?" "Spiritually, where do you want to be in three years?" They've found that people with personal goals are more committed to improving their workplaces.[10] Do you ask prospective employees or docents questions as searching as these?

If you don't have the right kind of people in your key visitor-service jobs, try to move them to another job better suited to their skills. One study of a British company found that nearly fifty percent of the people in customer-facing teams were not suited for that role.[11] One way to make sure you hire people with the right skills is to have them try out the job for a day.

At Central Market in Austin, Texas, applicants go through a five-step screening process including a group interview called "Taste of the Future." They are given information about the company, including a straightforward view of the grocery business, which includes the expectation that they'll work holidays and weekends. They also do practical exercises in teams, like putting together a display from a basket of groceries, then "selling" it to the interviewers. They are encouraged to

Pret a Manger is a successful chain of fresh-food shops in the UK. Applicants who pass two screening interviews then spend a "Pret experience day" working in one of the shops. Afterward, the staff members in the shop vote on whether to hire that applicant. Ninety-five percent of Pret applicants are not hired. The five percent who make it are amazing.[12]

leave the screening interview at any time if they realize Central Market isn't right for them. Out of sixteen or so applicants, one or two usually leave. The ones who are hired often stay for years.[13]

At the San Diego Zoo the interview for the coveted educator-guide positions includes an on-the-spot interpretive talk. The candidates have been given information about an animal in advance. During the interview, they're handed the animal and asked to tell a "tour group" about it. They're rated on both their interpretive skills and their rapport with the animal.

Customer service skills can be nurtured

You might think that exceptional companies have hard-core customer-service training programs. They do, but training is seen as a privilege, not a punishment. They pair new hires with great employees for on-the-job modeling. But one thing is more important than any lecture or video (although those play a part): exceptional companies invest time in their new hires. Stanley Steemer gives each new employee a "passport" for visiting eight top executives for one-on-one meetings. The new hires see that they are important enough to warrant top executives' time, and the executives remain connected with and committed to their employees.[14] At Disney both departmental trainers and front-line staff are involved with training new hires, who come out of Disney's Traditions orientation training believing that they can make a difference to the company.[15] Do new hires at your site spend any time with your executive director, board members, or upper managers?

Go easy on rules. Great companies share another trait in employee training: they don't bombard their workers with rules. The Nordstrom employee handbook used to be simply a small card that stated "Use your good judgment in all situations."[16] The Ritz Carlton Hotels use the in-house motto "Ladies and gentlemen serving ladies and gentlemen."[17] Some companies make repetitive training sessions (like safety drills) fun by turning them into games or competitions. They also encourage and reward risk taking, since employees who feel empowered give better customer service, which improves profits.

When your staff speaks, listen. Perhaps most important, great companies value the input of front-line staff, with sayings like "The front line can't lie."[18] At many top companies management stays in touch with the front line by working with customers every quarter (Pret a Manger), helping out during the holiday season by manning the phones or packing boxes (amazon.co.uk), or simply walking around talking to customers and employees (CEO Richard Branson, Virgin Atlantic). Some companies locate their board of directors' offices next to the customer-service department (Financial Times Group) in order to underscore the manager-employee relationship.[19] Your site could incorporate this key step by having top management and board members work special events or spend time out on the floor on a regular basis. At the Cerritos Library in California, everyone on the staff rotates through the front "concierge desk" for thirty-minute shifts. In addition, library staffers roam the floors, actively seeking out visitors who need assistance.[20]

Connect people to numbers. Last, companies create great, committed employees by keeping no financial secrets. They share the numbers that relate customer satisfaction to profitability, so that employees understand why customer service is so important. When employees feel valued and want to succeed, they care about the bottom line. On its intranet U.S. office supply giant Staples has included an easy way for employees to submit ideas for improving profits. Since the company added this feature, employee suggestions have tripled, and Staples estimates a savings of $200 million after making use of those suggestions.[21] Do you actively solicit and implement ideas from your front-line employees?

Remember that if your organization loses visitors or guests, it's very likely because of an uncaring attitude from a staff member.[22] Eighty percent of profits usually come from only about twenty percent of your customers.[23] So it's critical that all your employees understand the role they play in a great visitor experience—every day, for every visitor.

Eighty percent of profits usually come from only about twenty percent of your customers.

People first

The most successful businesses value employees over profits, over executives, even over serving the community. Nordstrom's organizational chart is an inverted pyramid, with customers at the top and front-line staff next in priority.[24] This is very different from the standard organizational chart, with the executives at the top and front-line staff at the bottom. The New York Aquarium also uses an inverted-pyramid approach.

Larger businesses are usually split into departments or teams on their organizational charts. Those departments may, over time, become the focus for employees. Rather than serving the visitor, they are "making the food-service budget" or "meeting marketing goals." It's important for everyone to remember that, in the eyes of your visitor, departments are arbitrary divisions. At a large urban zoo, each department has developed its own uniform, with bus drivers in one color polo shirt, educators in another color, animal keepers in khaki, and so on. While this may help staff feel pride in their departments, it also supports departmental rivalries. And zoo visitors only want to know one thing: "Do you work here?"

Southwest Airlines believes that employees should be educated about the company, because the more they know, the more they care.[25] An empowered staff is your greatest asset, as it creates a sense of ownership in your business. According to a 2003 study, absenteeism—some of it due to apathy—costs companies $800 per worker every year.[26] Happy employees are more productive and more loyal. Employee satisfaction also lowers your costs, as you spend less money recruiting and training replacements, with less downtime as new hires get up to speed. A recent study showed that replacing employees costs at least a third of their annual salary.[27] Nonprofit staff members have a specialized skill set, so the cost to replace them is closer to half their annual pay.

The cost to replace nonprofit workers is half their annual salary.

It's important to hold on to your employees for another reason. Experts are predicting a skilled worker shortage in the U.S. and abroad. This shortage will be due to greater numbers of Baby Boomers retiring, with fewer highly skilled college and high school graduates appearing to take their places.[28] If you need talent, consider looking to the growing pool of recently retired people who may want a second career.[29]

Work spaces

How do you keep your employees happy and committed? Start with the workspace. Job satisfaction and workplace design are closely connected.[30] A pioneering firm in workplace design and research is BOSTI (Buffalo Organization for Social and Technological Information). According to BOSTI, a well-designed office increases worker productivity by five to nine percent.[31] Workers need to perform without distractions and with enough "acoustic privacy" to focus on their tasks. Fully enclosed offices are much better than cubicles for encouraging good employee communication, even though it might seem counterintuitive. When workers are constantly listening to others' conversations, it distracts them, and their productivity drops. Enclosed spaces don't need to be large; BOSTI found that small, but acoustically private, offices between fifty and sixty square feet are sufficient to increase productivity, communication, learning, a sense of teamwork, and job satisfaction.[32]

Beauty and the bottom line. People work better in attractive environments. Workspaces should be clean, comfortable, and welcoming. When I see some behind-the-scenes areas at groceries, hardware stores, and hotels, I am not surprised at the low employee morale I see out front. Some employees-only spaces are dirty, with ugly cinderblock walls, ripped carpeting, and no amenities. A 1950s study found that workers in an ugly room (versus a neutral or beautiful one) rushed through their work, wanted to skip work, and complained of fatigue, headaches, and irritability.[33] Museums are notorious for putting staff offices in substandard spaces, often relegating desks and people to basements, closets, and even old bathrooms.

Can you paint the walls or add area rugs? Let your employees choose the wall colors? Allow them to paint or decorate their own workspaces? Can you put real art on the walls by finding local artists who want exposure, contacting local high schools or colleges who want a real-world project for their students, or encouraging creative employees to come up with decor? No one enjoys coming to a beige cubicle every day; there are many esthetically appealing and affordable options available for storage and decoration. If you can't afford to cover all the costs, can you give everyone a day's pay to clean, paint, and decorate workspaces themselves? Or can you at least buy the pizza while your staff members upgrade their offices on a day off?

Invest in your staff

Pay them to learn. Encourage them to share their knowledge. Workers represent eighty-two percent of the cost of doing business.[34] Even if you aren't able to reimburse their fees, encouraging them to attend a conference or training on paid time shows that you are invested in their growth. Set up a time for them to share what they've learned with other employees to foster an atmosphere of learning. If you have an employee intranet, invest in online training; it's a great way to support your employees. In Germany, METRO Group's intranet has a "Knowledge Quest" game to teach employees advanced retailing concepts.[35]

Perks and rewards

Companies with big budgets provide amazing perks like workout facilities, on-site childcare, and stock options. Even if your organization can't afford that level of perk, there are many other ways you can show employees your appreciation.

The pamper-profitability connection. I once worked at a museum that was planning a huge expansion. The staff at every level was overworked and exhausted. We used to joke about how we *all* needed makeovers. And we did. No one had time to get a haircut or go to the gym, and we all looked pretty frayed. If all your employees look ragged, it's a sign that they aren't taking care of themselves and that morale may be low. Try to encourage healthy behaviors and other types of self-care like haircuts and massages. Perhaps you can trade tickets with a spa or alternative healthcare provider to make these services available as employee perks.

Can you make a room available for an exercise class or a Weight Watchers meeting at lunchtime or after hours? Can you set up a regular time (like payday) for chair massages? Reward employees with comp time, and adopt an open policy about mental-health days. Instead of requiring employees to lie when they need a day off, encourage them to take a mental-health day as a reward for hard work. Instead of slacking off, your renewed and trusted employees will work even harder for you.

Some companies have a strong tradition of celebration and are known for their great parties. Celebrate any and all occasions: birthdays, good visitor feedback, holidays, and revenue goals reached. (And be sure that you officially note any sad or difficult milestones as well.) In the UK a mobile phone company called O2 has the "O2 Fun Zone" on their intranet, where employees send each other e-cards to celebrate notable occasions.[36] Celebrate the achievements of hard-working employees by giving them nice send-offs when they decide to leave you. Nothing is more demoralizing to other employees than seeing someone work hard for fifteen years and then get treated like a traitor for deciding to move on.

How will these ideas work at your site? Regardless of the size of your staff or your budget, you can put people first. Anything you can do to encourage your employees' passion and positive attitudes will bring you rewards in productivity and profits. The exercises on pages 167–68 will help you rate how you're doing and suggest ways you can further invest in your most important resource, your staff. Now that we have your foundation in place, we'll begin the next section—looking at your site from your visitor's point of view.

Your site

BREAKING IT DOWN

In Section 1, I talked about how our economy has changed and how our world is now experience driven. In Section 2 you learned more about your visitors: what they want from your organization, how to influence them in your favor, and how to shape your brand to support your experience. We examined the critical importance of your staff members in creating a memorable experience. You may have already done some of the exercises from Sections 1 and 2 with your Experience*ology* team to improve your understanding of how visitors relate to your organization. Now it's time to look at your site itself—from your visitor's point of view.

Whether you are an employee or a volunteer at your site, you have probably arrived there hundreds, maybe even thousands, of times. It's hard to remember what it's like to visit for the first time—when you didn't know your way around, when you had to pay to get in, when you had to come in the main entrance or find the front door from down the block. Taking a fresh look is critical to improving your visitor experience, because it will lead you to change old habits. On page 142, I suggest enlisting some experience testers—preferably people who have never visited your site before—to help you look at things with new eyes.

Whatever your field—art, history, botany, zoology, conservation, education, or science—you have your own vocabulary. You know how to behave at your site, what to wear, and how noisy or quiet to be. In order to draw new visitors to your site, you'll need to take a big step back and look at your organization from the perspective of someone who isn't "one of you."

How do you go about changing what you offer? Where do you begin? All organizations have limited time, staff, and money for making changes. Experience*ology* takes a step-by-step approach, breaking the visitor experience down into eight sequential steps. It allows you to analyze each area of your site, decide where you can and should improve, and develop a plan for making changes. Keep in mind that there is some overlap in the steps, but they've been designed to help you examine your experience in manageable chunks. The overall goal is to create a greater connection between your visitors and your site. Even small, inexpensive changes like a paint job can make a big difference. Here are the steps that we'll take in the next eight chapters:

1. Invitation

The invitation step begins when a potential visitor says, "Let's do something today." It ends when he arrives in your parking lot and spies your front door.

2. Welcome

The welcome step begins at your entrance and ends when the visitor has had contact with someone who works for you.

3. Orientation

When the visitor moves away from your greeter, the orientation step begins. It ends when he decides what to do first.

4. Comfort

The comfort step is found throughout your site. It's designed in—to permanent structures, built-ins, seating, exhibits or displays, and signs.

5. Communication

Everything you convey in written or spoken words is included in the communication step.

6. Sensation

When you're designing your experience or setting up visitors' interaction with your staff, always remember to ask, "Is it fun?" "Does it engage all five senses?" and "Is it unexpected?"

7. Common sense

The common-sense step provides smarter, more logical, more efficient ways to run your business. It includes using visitor studies, applying trends, realigning your mission if necessary, and collaborating with like-minded organizations.

8. Finale

The finale is everything a visitor leaves with, both tangible and intangible.

CHAPTER 7

Designing an invitation for your guests

Step #1: Invitation
The invitation step begins when a potential visitor says, "Let's do something today."
It ends when he arrives in your parking lot and spies your front door.

Imagine going to your mailbox and finding invitations to the following events: a buddy's fiftieth birthday bash in Vegas; a posh wedding at a swanky hotel; a Super Bowl chili cook-off; a glossy art gallery opening; a six-year-old's soccer-themed birthday party across the street; a black-and-white gala fundraiser; and the grand opening of a new car dealership.

Each of those invitations is quite different, and you were probably able to see each one in your mind, perhaps because you've actually received similar invitations. Depending on who you are, some of those invitations would excite you, and others wouldn't interest you at all. Some might go straight into the recycling bin while others would be tacked up on the fridge. The style and content of each of those invitations give you a lot of information. You understand how long the event will be, what to wear, what to bring, who else might be there, how much time it will take to get there, and what you might be doing. The invitation spells out what kind of experience you will have if you attend.

A hand-addressed invitation to a black-tie party—perhaps wrapped in a polka-dot ribbon—sets up different expectations from the ones evoked by a Day-Glo flyer stuffed into your mailbox. The invitation to the gala is more personal, was done with more care, and is on nicer paper—all of which combines to make a stronger statement of quality. Similarly, the way you invite visitors to your site is the first important step in providing them with a seamless, stellar visitor experience. Some organizations operate on the assumption that "If we build it, they will come." (How many expensive museum expansion projects have been able to sustain second-year attendance?) But attendance is not magic, and visitors need to be wooed. Your invitation is the first step.

Reaching your target visitors

The first aspect of developing an effective invitation is to consider your "guests." Who do you want to visit your site? If you've already completed the branding exercises for Chapter 5, you have an excellent and very specific idea of your target visitors. You want to include everyone on your guest list who might want to come and stop inviting people who aren't interested. If you want to draw teenage girls to your Girls in Science camp, your invitation will look and feel quite different from the one you send to families with preschool children for a storybook hour at your children's museum or library. I'm not suggesting that you are trying to exclude anyone, but sites often design their invitations for "everyone" instead of focusing their resources on appealing to the most likely visitors and growing from there. Keep your target visitors in mind throughout this chapter.

In Chapter 5, I mentioned a podiatrist who worked with consultant Jon Schallert. The podiatrist wanted to know how to narrow her marketing efforts to get the best value for her money. Once she realized that she was focusing on active sportswomen in the forty-to-eighty-year age group, her invitation became much clearer and more effective.

Logoland, here we come

The foundation of your organization's identity is your logo. In addition to declaring your site's name, your logo should convey its personality, using typeface, color, word, and symbol.[1] Use your logo consistently on everything you print as well as on your Web site. You can also use your logo in creative ways at your facility.

But *which* logo? Some organizations are in the unfortunate position of having more than one logo, which confuses visitors and dilutes the site's brand. This often happens with gardens, aquariums, or zoos that have a research arm or a governing society. The research arm or society often has a separate name and its own logo. From the public's point of view, these divisions are artificial and confusing. It can create fundraising challenges if you don't have a well-defined identity. One logo and one name are best.

Departments within a large organization often create their own materials, and over time those pieces can develop lives of their own. Take time to step back, collect a sample of everything that's going out to your public, and see if they are consistent.[2] The usual ways of inviting people to your site—through advertising and marketing, print pieces, and Web sites—should all be coordinated. Frequently, though, the only consistent aspect of all of these is a logo. While you don't want every communication to look the same, consider each piece you produce as one part of a coordinated suite of invitations that will help convey your site's personality and build your brand.

Fine tune your phone voice. Check to be sure that your voice-mail system is welcoming and reflects your brand image. Complicated voice-mail trees are irritating to visitors and expensive to you if they don't work efficiently. Visitors stuck in your voice-mail system are using precious minutes if you pay for incoming calls on a toll-free number.[3] And make sure callers can reach a human being easily by pressing "0" at any time.

Party planners unite

What about special events? For those, you will be designing actual printed invites. Keep in mind the specific audience you want to draw to your event and what information they need in order to make the decision to attend. Special events are a great way to attract new audiences to your site. But if the atmosphere at your gala occasions is very different from your usual vibe, keep in mind that some visitors may not come again until you hold another similar event. Museums' audiences for special events are often different from the regular museum audience, because these festive occasions allow visitors social interaction, a comfortable environment, and active participation,[4] rewards that may not be available during regular hours.

Speak designer-ese like a pro

The best way to create a strong organizational identity is to hire a graphic designer to develop it with you. An "identity" combines your logo with a visual design system, including typeface, colors, imagery, and a specific editorial tone, all complementing your organization's personality.[5] Share the answers to any exercises you complete for

Chapters 1 through 5 with your designer. He or she will build on that work to develop your identity; a good designer can bring many ideas and elements together into one strong look that tells your story.

Spend as much as you can afford when you're working with a designer. Smaller firms and independent designers have lower overhead and are less expensive than large companies. Nonprofits that are strapped for cash can sometimes get design work donated. In that case, approach a larger firm that can afford to do some pro bono work, and keep that firm in mind when you have a paying job, like a grant-funded project, later. Design schools and local colleges are often happy to have real-world projects for their students to work on. In any case, the more prepared you are as a client (by following the recommendations below), the easier and faster the organizational-identity process will be. By getting prepared in advance you'll save money if you are paying a designer, and you won't waste the time of a designer who's working pro bono.

I asked a group of designers for suggestions on how to create a smooth working relationship. Clients who are well prepared and clearly understand the scope of the work rank highest with the designers I canvassed. They favor clients who have clear goals for an identity program but don't have preconceived notions of what the result will look like. Designers need your input; they will ask you to describe your organization, giving relevant details but avoiding superlatives. If there are design constraints, like elements of an old logo that must be incorporated, be clear about that up front.

Clearly define the scope of the project before you get bids.[6] Designer Tanya Bredehoft suggests that a prepared client would have answered the following questions before meeting with a designer. With these questions addressed ahead of time, any client-designer relationship is off to a clean, fast start:

- 1. Who is your target audience? (youth, preschoolers, families, etc.)
- 2. What are you trying to accomplish with the design?
- 3. What image of your site do you want to project to your target audience? (family-oriented, educational, recreational, etc.)
- 4. What's your budget?
- 5. What's your timeframe?[7]

At the end of the project, the designer should provide you with an identity-standards manual. This would include your new logo and any variations, the color palette and typeface(s) to be used, tag lines and additional copy, images that may be part of the system, and any sound and animation guidelines for Web and broadcast applications.[8] You should also have the designer create templates for flyers, business cards, a letterhead, and other printed material like coupons or brochures. Make sure the designer understands what type of computer software and fonts you have, so you can use the new templates easily.

Designers from MAYA Design created templates for several types of signs for the Carnegie Library in Pittsburgh. These templates are linked to the library's intranet, so authorized users can log in, insert updated information in the correct fields, and print the signs on special paper. This clever system allows the library to get fresh information out on the floor in a matter of minutes, while maintaining the library's design standards.[9]

A trail of bread crumbs to your site

Now that you have a strong identity in place, consider how visitors will find you. It's important to review every aspect of their trip to your door. Look at the street signs and those for public transportation near your site and decide what you might add that gives people clear directions to your entrance and parking area. In some cases city, county, provincial, or state regulations dictate the look of any signs you add. However, the governing authority will sometimes allow you to use signs of your own design if you follow size and placement guidelines. Whatever you can do to create a consistent look is good; it strengthens your brand identity. But any kind of directional signage, even if it's highway brown, is part of your invitation and helps visitors find you.

P is for parking

The parking lot is an important and often neglected part of the visitor experience. Make sure yours is clean and free of litter. For the majority of visitors, the first impression of your site begins when they park. Difficulties with parking—limited meter time, high rates, inadequate

For the majority of visitors, the first impression of your site begins when they park.

spaces—all affect the length of a visitor's stay and his decision to come again. While many of these issues might be out of your hands, get out and review your parking. Brainstorming affordable ways to improve it can be an illuminating experience.

If you have a dedicated parking lot, your identity system should be an integral part of the signage there. At the very least, a clearly identified parking area is crucial to a good visitor experience. For large lots, a parking-lot greeter during busy times helps create a welcoming environment and makes efficient use of the space.

Where's my car? Creative solutions to finding one's car are always helpful. Men respond to letters and numbers, women remember colors, and kids like animals, fruit, and symbols.[10] These section identifiers can incorporate your subject matter. At a garage for an electronics research firm in Zurich, the designers used a famous scientist for each letter, creating a mini-interpretive panel—with a photo, some information, and an identifying color—for people to read while they waited for the elevator.[11] Just keep any text short and simple; people don't want to spend more time in parking lots than they have to.[12] Smaller parking lots can also be tied in thematically. At COPIA, the wine-country museum in Sonoma, California, parking-lot dividers are planted with grapevines.

Be sure that the theme of your parking lot doesn't interfere with people finding your front door. At the Chicago Botanic Garden, the architect created green "rooms" for parking instead of a huge expanse of concrete. It was lovely, but visitors frequently had no idea how to find the entrance to the garden itself. It was not uncommon to see people walking away from the entrance as they wandered the rooms in search of the garden. It was not the best way to start a visit.

The perfect invitation. In the end, an ideal invitation for your site welcomes potential guests and targets your most likely visitors. It helps you get the most from your precious resources and clearly conveys what kind of experience you have to offer. A great invitation is unmistakable when visitors see it. The exercises on page 170 will help you design your invitation. In the next chapter we'll consider how you welcome your visitors once you've successfully attracted them to your site.

CHAPTER 8

Dust off your first impression

Step #2: Welcome
The welcome step begins at your entrance and ends when the visitor has had contact with someone who works for you.

On the wind-whipped, craggy coast of northern California is a town called Trinidad. When you arrive at the Lost Whale Bed & Breakfast, one of the first things you hear is a deep, sonorous wind chime. Since there's always a sea breeze, the chime is constantly tolling, reminding you of whalers and lighthouses and mystery. I still think of the Lost Whale whenever I hear a deep chime like that. If I ever find the right one, I'm going to buy it for our garden.

Back here in sunny San Diego, the entrance to San Diego's Mingei International Museum is unmistakable. Twelve-foot-tall fantasy animal sculptures by artist Nikki de Saint-Phalle are covered in mosaics of colorful tile and bits of mirror, glinting in the sun. Kids are usually climbing on these figures, while tourists use them as a photo opportunity. They herald the gorgeous and colorful folk art inside the museum.

At Extraordinary Desserts just a few blocks away, an elegant sign hanging perpendicular to the sidewalk lets you know you're in for a treat. The company's name, in sophisticated script lettering, creates anticipation, while the plantings in front of the sign match the acid-green and olive logo. You pass a pretty courtyard on the way to the front door, where luscious cakes decorated with fresh flowers and gold leaf beckon as soon as you step inside.

There's no doubt that a strong welcome builds on your invitation, shaping your visitor's impression of the experience she's about to receive. The next time you go to a high-end grocery store, like Trader Joe's or Whole Foods, notice that they usually mass fresh flowers at the entrance, with mounds of colorful produce just beyond. Compare that to the impression you might get at a convenience store, where beer signs, cigarette posters, and lottery tickets scream for your attention. If your site were a grocery store, which kind would you be?

Fabulous front doors

Whether you are an indoor or outdoor facility, you have a "front door." In outdoor spaces, gateways are the transition point, delineating "outside" and "inside." Portals are places where people can stop and consider their options.[1] Your front door should tell a potential visitor, from about half a block away, where and who you are. It should be commanding enough to inspire someone to visit on impulse, as well as familiar enough to signal visitors that they've found you.[2]

Up your rating. Plant a tree. Trees planted by your entrance increase the positive impression of your facility. Larger trees, pruned properly to allow people to see your signage, have the highest ratings in consumer research studies. In these studies, people were shown photos of buildings with and without trees or plants out front. Without ever going inside, customers rated businesses with trees as more appealing and comfortable, better maintained, and offering better service and products. Customers said they would be willing to pay more for shaded parking, and about ten percent more for products from stores with trees out front![3]

An unmistakable welcome, seen at a glance. Make sure your main entrance captures people's attention as they walk or drive by, as visitors might not approach you from head on. Some sites, like the Mingei International Museum, use oversize icons to play with scale. Others, like Extraordinary Desserts, use colored awnings and a fancy sign to do the job. Depending on your site's personality, maybe a 3-D sign bursting through the front wall is appropriate.[4]

Window displays must work from a distance of six feet away. If you have display windows on the street, follow retail researcher Paco Underhill's advice: Keep it simple. Make it big. Signs in your windows should be no more than two or three words long. And consider how different light levels and glare from the sun will affect the display.[5]

Some museums have forbidding entrances, with marble steps and imposing columns. If this sounds like your site, what can you do to soften the architecture? Make sure that the mechanics of your front door

Customers said they would be willing to pay more for shaded parking, and about ten percent more for products from stores with trees out front!

are welcoming as well. Can someone actually get it open? Some front doors are ridiculously heavy; it's like you're breaking an airlock on the Starship Enterprise. Not only are easy-to-open doors friendly, but they also follow guidelines for accessibility.[6] Limit the information on your front door to basics like your name and your hours of operation. People only spend about two seconds reading signs on doorways as they pass through.[7] A nice touch is to use a symbol from your logo in a repeated pattern if you need a safety decal on a glass door.[8]

Advance organizers

An "advance organizer" is visual shorthand for what will follow.[9] While the term originated in the field of education, the technique is used in many places. City Wok, a restaurant in Chicago, has a huge rice bowl and chopsticks protruding from the building's facade. *Chocolate*, a traveling exhibition designed by the Field Museum in Chicago, featured an entry wall made to look like a box of chocolates.[10] Three video screens played interviews of people talking about chocolate, and you could perch on a stool designed to look like a chocolate cupcake. Advance organizers like these effectively broadcast to potential visitors what they will find inside. Providing advance organizers helps visitors better understand your offerings.[11]

A friendly first impression

Just inside your front door is your visitor's first impression. Do they see fresh paint, fresh merchandise in your store, and fresh signs? Or a torn, dirty hodgepodge of messages tacked up on a pitted bulletin board, behind a front desk as fortress-like as a World War II bunker? Stand in your entryway a moment and study what you are presenting to your visitors as a first impression. You may have passed by it so many times that you don't truly see it anymore.

Who do you see?

Once your visitor is inside the doors, who is the first person she sees? In many cases, it is a security guard. I appreciate the role security plays. I have thoroughly enjoyed working with some great security people over the years. But even the nicest security guard sends a strong message to your visitors. In the case of a bank, it might be the right message: "Don't rob us, I have a gun." But you might not want to say "We don't trust you" before you say anything else.

Another problem with security guards is that they're often contract employees hired and trained by an outside company. If that's the case at your site, talk to your contractor to see how you can get involved in choosing and training the people who work in this critical role at your site. You'll be pleasantly surprised to find that many security guards are choosing to work for you because they're interested in what you offer. Make the most of that resource.

Uniforms

At state and national parks, rangers often have multiple duties, with security just one of them. Unfortunately, they have to wear the uniform and carry the gun. Keep reminding security staff during trainings and meetings that some audiences are sensitive to uniformed personnel, and to overcompensate with friendliness. (Here in San Diego, a park ranger I know went to a grade school to do a presentation. To some of the kids his uniform looked exactly like the border patrol, and they promptly burst into tears, terrified of him. Crying kids are not receptive to an educational program!)

Uniforms can relate to the theme of your organization and, if used creatively, can help make a positive impression. At the National Cowboy and Western Heritage Museum in Oklahoma City, Oklahoma, the security guards wear leather vests, deputy stars, cowboy hats, and boots. The whole effect is friendly and fun—in character with the site. At the Living Room restaurant in Seminyak, Bali, the waitresses all wear custom-made floral shift dresses in a variety of complementary color combinations: simple, lovely, and striking. At Jungle Roots Children's Dentistry in Arizona, the front-desk staff wear sweater twin-sets—pale lime green on Mondays and Wednesdays, and turquoise on Tuesdays and Thursdays—combined with black pants. This classy combo matches the decor, doesn't look like a "uniform," and still presents a unified image as part of the brand.

Volunteer greeters

Another challenge many nonprofits face is having volunteers, rather than paid workers, staff their front desks. I love and appreciate volunteers. Most nonprofits couldn't function without them. Many are delightful, friendly people who dedicate themselves to serving an institution. I've also worked with a few volunteers who were not exactly "people persons." Some I might describe as cranky or intimidating, not welcoming.

Even if you're not able to afford a paid staff person at your front desk, consider carefully and hire right for that position. Make sure that friendly people skills are part of that volunteer's job description and training. At one museum I visited, there was both a scary guard and a crabby greeter in a tiny, airless foyer. Yikes! While it is a delicate business to shift or retrain long-time volunteers, you can't afford to make a bad first impression on your visitors. At the new Seattle Public Library, friendly volunteer greeters roam near the entrance to help visitors feel welcome and find what they're looking for.[12] For more suggestions on managing and training volunteers, see Further Reading, on page 171.

Making your welcome crew work for you

At the Tampa Art Museum in Florida, an outside contractor provides security, with a guard placed in each of the galleries. While those guards know everyone on the staff, they are not included in any staff functions or training. Because of their key front-line positions, the guards can give you a complete "visitor profile"—tell you how much time people spend in the galleries, what the top attractions are, whether the museum has enough bathrooms, and what people complain about. The guard I spoke to knew every artifact in his gallery and could tell me which docents made mistakes on tours. That guard probably has a better idea of the museum's visitor experience than someone high up in the front office, who might only visit the galleries when showing donors around.

While there might be some tricky logistics involved, try to include security guards and front-desk staff people in interpretive training about your exhibits. Ask the security contractor if you may choose guards with outgoing, service-based personalities to work at your site. Elicit their feedback regularly about what visitors are saying. Invite them to staff parties so they feel connected to the institution.

The same goes for gardeners, custodial staff, and retail or restaurant staff. Every single person who comes into contact with your visitors should be hired for their customer-service mindset, informed about your business, and trained in customer-service techniques. It's your job to help them understand what a critical role they play in creating your brand experience.

A special welcome on special days

If you have developed a program aimed at a particular market segment, consider using a special welcome crew on those days. The Monterey Bay Aquarium in California has a marketing coordinator for the Latino audience. For one of their special programs, Día del Niño, kids twelve and under get free admission and are met by a mariachi band.[13] Other sites use costumed characters, musicians, and themed decorations to set a welcoming mood. A Cajun restaurant in Chicago, Heaven on Seven, uses balloons, streamers, and confetti to welcome visitors during Mardi Gras season.

The exercises on page 172 will help you analyze and improve your welcome, from front door to front desk to the staff members who greet your visitors. In the next chapter we'll cover how to orient your visitors so they feel comfortable in your space and can make the most of your offerings.

CHAPTER 9

Lost in space

Step #3: Orientation
When the visitor moves away from your greeter, the orientation step begins. It ends when he decides what to do first.

I can think of a number of times when I've been well and truly lost. When you're driving in Chile, you have to know that a certain road eventually goes to a particular town, because there are no route markers on the roads themselves. At a state park in Kentucky if you miss the sign for Prospector's Trail on a hike, you end up miles from where you need to be. On a street corner in London, with tiny streets going off at all angles, you can't see the next intersection, so even a good map can't help you.

Feeling lost is frustrating, tiring, and sometimes scary. Fear of getting lost can prevent people from visiting outdoor sites like parks.[1] Large, confusing indoor sites like some very big museums can be a bad experience and keep people from visiting again. You don't want your visitors feeling disoriented when they visit you.

Effective orientation helps your visitors enjoy spending time at your site, pay more attention to what you have to offer, and need less help from staff members to find their way around. This chapter shows you how to improve your orientation, so that visitors aren't lost in your space.

The transition zone

Retail anthropologist Paco Underhill discovered the phenomenon of the transition zone during years of study.[2] As people enter your site, there is a short period of adjustment. Their eyes get used to the new lighting conditions while their bodies react to changes in temperature, sight, and sound. They are scanning with all five senses, taking it all in. And then finally they land. Now they are really *in*. Until they land, anything you have offered them is completely wasted. That includes any signs, flyers, or interactions with staff. The size of the transition zone is different at every site.

Slow is beautiful. You want your transition zone to be as shallow as possible, so you can devote more space to your offerings. Automatic doors or wide-open doorways increase the length of your transition zone, as there is nothing to slow visitors down, and you *want* to slow them down and help them make the transition into your space. Having a sound at the entrance, whether it's the squeak of hinges, a fountain, or some other aural cue helps narrow the zone. Changes in lighting level also help. Many retail stores use a "power display," a table facing the door piled with shirts or sweaters. This functions like a speed bump to make people change their stride and gets them to stop and touch some merchandise. Power displays are not intended to sell things, but to act as an advance organizer (introduced in Chapter 8)—something to tell people what they will find in the store. You could offer a similar speed bump by setting up a simple display case with visuals and objects only, no interpretive text.

Although it's not good to have a greeter accost visitors the second they walk in, a staff person stationed near the door can help shorten the transition zone. As soon as he sees a person "land," the greeter can give a brief welcome and offer the visitor something appropriate like a map or a coupon to use later. If you have a retail store, staff contact is important for another reason. People buy more when they interact with staff members.[3] The more contact visitors have with your staff, the more time they spend "shopping," that is, interacting with exhibits.

At busy sites it's especially important to help people make the transition quickly. Otherwise you'll have a mass of people clogging up your entryway. At the San Diego Zoo, visitors come through a dark ticketing breezeway, maps in hand, and emerge into a sunny plaza. Buses are driving by, crowds are passing in both directions, there are animals to see. Photographers want to take people's pictures, and shops on either side are vying for their attention. Tucked off to the left is a welcome booth staffed by friendly volunteers. If the zoo moved the booth so that it faced the entryway, visitors who needed help could more easily see it, and the congestion of this very busy transition zone might be lessened. Shopping is not the first thing you want to do when you arrive at a zoo. Nor do you want to be pounced on by a photographer. Shifting the shop signs out of the transition zone and moving the photographers to another location, like near a queue, could also help clear up the congestion.

The right-hand bias

In the early 1990s the Chicago Botanic Garden built a gorgeous new visitor center, housing a café, gift shop, plant-information center, and orientation room designed as an advance organizer. Visitors walk from the parking lots through the visitor center into the gardens beyond. On the original plans, the orientation room was on the right-hand side as you walked through. Visitors would have been able to flow into the room to see small exhibits and a multimedia presentation about the garden. It would have been a nice place to wait for friends who were using the nearby restrooms.

But, for various reasons, the design was altered before construction; the orientation room ended up on the left and the plant-information center on the right. Few visitors ever crossed over to the left to visit the orientation room, so the money the garden spent on the room and the multimedia exhibits was wasted. On their way out, people blow right past the orientation room, intent on reaching the gift shop, the café, or the exit. People don't need orientation as they leave. In recent years the room has become rental space for special events.

Eyes right—and the feet follow. The planners should have remembered the importance of the right-hand bias in Western culture.[4] The most valuable real estate you have is in the right front corner of your site, just past the transition zone. People don't like to cross over to the left, so plan your site to take advantage of this bias. Since most people are right-handed, they also tend to reach right.[5] Consider this if you are designing elements that have handles or doors. At the renovated Carnegie Library in Pittsburgh, the self-checkout stations are on the right as you exit.[6]

You are here

Once your visitors have gotten through the transition zone, they are ready for orientation. There's an art to designing a good map. Most maps tend to be drawn in a plan, or straight-down, view. But people have an easier time understanding maps if they are drawn from an isometric (or 3-D) perspective.[7] This bird's-eye view shows elements drawn with some height and dimension to them, allowing the person using the map to visualize himself in the location. The Field Museum in Chicago combines a plan view with some notable elements drawn in 3-D, helping visitors recognize landmarks as they walk around.

Go ahead. The standard for maps used for driving is to place north at the top of the page. "You Are Here" maps are different. They should be oriented to the direction a person is facing, so "up" stretches out in front of him, regardless of where north is.[8] If you have "You Are Here" maps in several locations, each one should be oriented according to its unique location. If you have a stanchion with back-to-back maps, those maps should not be identical, as each side is facing a different direction. There are some lovely "You Are Here" maps in San Diego's Balboa Park, made of expensive porcelain enamel. Unfortunately, because they are all identical, at least half the time they are "wrong"—either upside-down or sideways—from the viewer's perspective.

Orient maps of outdoor sites with your front entrance at the bottom, as visitors will mentally place themselves according to where they parked. Indoors, Paco Underhill suggests placing "You Are Here" maps tabletop style, parallel to the floor at waist height, with icons on the map matching large icons hanging from ceilings or used on signage.[9] Tactile maps for visually impaired visitors can be a great addition. But make sure that bronze tactile maps aren't in the sun, or they get too hot to touch. Be aware that the star on "You Are Here" maps will get worn off, as nearly everyone touches it. Maps covered with a layer of Plexiglas, or ones with a raised bronze star, help reduce this kind of wear. At Cantigny Gardens in Illinois, a scale model of the gardens is visible under the floor, so you can walk around on top of it and learn about the site. This is a great permanent use for an expensive architectural model.

Map it out. Don't try to include everything on your map. Use light background shading on the areas you want to de-emphasize. Smooth out winding paths and simplify symbols. Label important features directly on the map rather than overdoing it with symbols. (But symbols are helpful for non-English readers, so balance their use depending on what percentage of your visitors speak other languages.)

Here's what your map should do:

- **1. Showcase your best features.** Include the most prominent and distinctive elements of your site.
- **2. Highlight decision points.** Show the main intersections in your site, where people must choose which direction to go.
- **3. Distinguish between areas that look similar.** If there are large areas that visitors might confuse, label them clearly.

Remember that maps suffer from information overload when too many people offer information. The visitor experience should take top priority in all map decisions, and any new map should be tested in prototype form with first-time visitors.[10]

Wayfinding

Wayfinding is defined as "signs and other graphics for visitor circulation."[11] These are the signs in the garden that direct you to the education center, the signs that send you to the right museum gallery, and the signs that get you to the outdoor café. Bad wayfinding can cost you money, as frustrated visitors leave without making a purchase.[12] A good wayfinding system is keyed to your map. It tells people where they are and what there is to do. If you have a large or complex site, hire a designer trained in environmental graphic design who has produced other wayfinding projects. Ideally, make an advance visit to a site designed by the person you are considering hiring. At your own site review any prototype signage, in place, from a distance. More than one expensive new library has had to redo their wayfinding signs because the beautiful, artsy font wasn't legible from across the hall. The best advice for large new building projects? Wait to install wayfinding until the building has been open for a while, and test, test, test.[13]

Be regional. Start by defining regions within your site. (You can add regions to an existing site.) Five, but no more than seven, regions are best.[14] Signal transitions from one area to another by changing the materials on signs, walls, and flooring. Name regions in simple terms that will make sense to your visitors: "Africa," "European Art," "Inventions," "Red Road." Keep the wording simple on wayfinding signs: the "Giant Panda Research Station" becomes "Pandas," the "MGM Grand Garden Arena" becomes "Grand Arena."

Wait to install wayfinding until the building has been open for a while, and test, test, test.

Create logical paths. Successful and visitor-friendly wayfinding systems work their magic by using a combination of graphic icons, names, and color coding. A great example is the Los Angeles Zoo, a complex site with paths winding over hilly terrain. The animal exhibits weren't organized by region, so the wayfinding team at Hunt Design came up with a brilliantly simple system. All the signage along each of the six main paths—like "Blue Avenue" or "Green Street"—is color coded to the map; visitors always know where they are.[15]

Review the placement and condition of all your signs on a regular basis, as temporary and obsolete signs have a way of mysteriously proliferating. Do you have a hodgepodge of signs that have been added over the years? You might try a zero-based approach to signage. (In zero-based budgeting you start from zero and add budget items, justifying the need for each as you go.) Remove all signs from an area, then add back only the ones you need to get the job done. Start on a computer. Take a digital photo of the area and, using a software program like PowerPoint, Photoshop, or Illustrator, remove each sign until you get to zero, then add signs back on your computer until you find the right balance. Sometimes you can combine several old signs into one well-designed new one.

Hand-lettered signs = red flag. Handwritten signs show only one thing: something isn't working, either in the design or operation of your site. Analyze the problem, talk to the staff member who put up the sign, and determine how best to fix it. Sometimes the problem isn't the lack of a sign, but a design flaw that needs to be addressed. One zoo's nocturnal exhibit has four different signs—posted in a cluster—all warning visitors to watch their step. It turns out that a hallway from bright sun into the dim "nocturnal" light was too short to permit a safe transition; people stumbled when they reached the ramp inside. Every time someone fell down, the zoo's legal department requested another warning sign—no way to solve a design problem.

Placement

You can have the greatest sign in the world, but if you put it in the wrong place, you've wasted your money and effort. Start with a digital photo of an area to try out size and placement. A mockup of every sign should be tested in place, because lighting conditions and location are so critical to effective signage. If you have several routes through your site, be sure to place signs on the lesser-used routes as well as the major ones, and in both directions of travel. If you have signs on movable stanchions, check to see that your cleaning crew replaces them correctly.[16] If not, someone on your staff might have to move them back into their proper places every single morning.

Make your signs pass the test. Sometimes placing signs head-on doesn't catch a visitor's attention. In that case, angle signs a bit so they're more visible as people are walking. Signs are most visible fifteen degrees above and below a standing adult's eye level.[17] It might be most convenient for you to review your site when it's closed, but you must test your sign placement when you're crowded too, under a variety of lighting conditions, and from a wheelchair, to make sure that key elements aren't blocked when the site is filled with visitors.

Watch their backs. Surround your signs and "You Are Here" maps with enough space for people to view them without being brushed from behind. Retail researcher Paco Underhill has discovered a phenomenon he calls "the butt-brush effect."[18] People in stores don't like to be brushed from behind while they're studying a product. (This includes brushing against one's purse or backpack.) If they get brushed several times, they will leave without buying. The phenomenon applies to people reading signs and studying maps, too. If they're crowded from behind, they'll leave without getting directions.

Help people go where *you* want them. The last trick about placement is to avoid the "shallow loop."[19] If you locate all your biggest draws right up front, people will simply loop through one end of your site and leave. Try placing something compelling at the back of your site to draw people in, then let the right-hand bias lead them out.

If you have an exhibit, sign, or product that isn't getting much attention, try to see what the problem is by observing how people behave in the problem area. Consider changing the placement of things they're ignoring—maybe moving a sign to the hallway next to the bathrooms or facing a queue. Visitors who are waiting are always grateful for something to do and will read just about anything. (But make sure the amount of information matches the speed at which the line moves. People get frustrated if you give them interesting information when they're moving too quickly to read it.) And before you place a new element, watch visitors to see what they are doing at the new location. A beautiful sign at the Woodland Park Zoo in Seattle was placed at a spot that seemed appropriate, but wasn't. Visitors approaching that spot had a decision to make about whether to turn right or left, so they all pulled out their maps and completely missed the sign.[20]

In the end, good orientation is a combination of great maps, well-designed signage, and sensible placement. With effective orientation tools your visitors will need less help from staff members to find their way around and will pay more attention to what you have to offer. Well-designed orientation works because it is comfortable for visitors to use. We'll look at other aspects of comfort in the next chapter.

CHAPTER 10

From toilets to typefaces

Step #4: Comfort
The comfort step is found throughout your site. It's designed in—to permanent structures, built-ins, seating, exhibits or displays, and signs.

You sink down into the cushions of a plush suede couch and cover yourself with a thick fleece throw. You're wearing your softest flannel shirt. In front of you is a plate of comfort food: meatloaf with mashed potatoes and gravy. Sounds pretty good, doesn't it? This chapter is about creating a thoroughly comfortable environment for your visitors.

Growing up, I loved visiting my friend Mona. Everything in her family's house felt welcoming. Comfort is as much about hospitality as it is about any particular attribute, like softness or cushioning. Mona's mom, a French Canadian gourmet cook, made real macaroni-and-cheese casseroles with good Swiss cheese and white wine, baked in the oven, along with more exotic fare like bouillabaisse. There were always fresh flowers on the table. Their house looks familiar now; just flip through the pages of *Martha Stewart Living* or a Pottery Barn catalog. But back in the 70s in my town, no one's house looked like that. They usually looked more like my friend Sharon's house down the street; her living-room furniture was encased in crinkly vinyl covers, with plastic runners laid down to protect the carpet. As much as I liked Sharon, I felt far more comfortable and welcome at Mona's house.

Why comfort is important— in body and mind

Research shows that the longer visitors stay at a site, the more time and money they spend.[1] Extending a customer's visit to a shopping mall from one hour to two makes her double her spending.[2] If you can offer food, shopping, services, or entertainment, people will stay longer and spend more. The more comfortable they feel, the longer they'll stay. This builds on what we covered in Section 2; it's most cost efficient to sell more goods and services to your existing visitors than it is to draw in new ones.[3] I'm going to talk about comfort in two sections, "body comfort" and "mind comfort." Body comfort is about the physical needs of your visitors: food, seating, or restrooms. Mind comfort is about your visitors' psychological needs—their feelings of safety, security, and ease.

Body comfort

In the 1950s, a psychologist named Abraham Maslow developed a theory called the Hierarchy of Needs. It was illustrated by a pyramid with the bottom levels representing core physical needs like food, shelter, and safety. Maslow believed that these basic needs had to be met before a person could even think about meeting higher needs, like the one for socializing. My friends know that if I start getting really hungry, we've got to stop what we're doing and feed me some protein. I can't focus or function very well otherwise. That need speaks more loudly than any fun we might be having. Humans are constantly moving up and down the pyramid of needs throughout the course of a day, satisfying hunger, staying warm—and then being social or doing something educational.[4]

Basic human needs have to be met before a person can focus on acquiring knowledge, appreciating esthetics, or even enjoying shopping. Those are all higher-level needs. Some of your visitors might be able to push through their discomfort, but they won't enjoy the experience as much as they would if you had met their basic needs. That's why you must make sure your visitors are as comfortable as possible at your site. At the Pueblo Grande Museum in Phoenix, Arizona, a rack of umbrellas is waiting for visitors, either to protect them during desert downpours or to provide shade from the blazing sun during their mile-long walk around the mound outdoors.

Seating

In Chapter 1 we saw how serious the Nordstrom department store chain is about their seating. But it's not just stores that should care about it. If there is a chance that someone might need or want to sit down while they are visiting, you should think about seating. If a couple comes into an exhibition but the content appeals to only one person, you need a bench. If you don't provide enough seating, people will perch on railings, planters, fixtures, exhibit cases, and shelves. If you have a large site where people will be walking a great deal, you need to plan for seating. If people are tired, you lose them, both mentally and physically.

> "I love seating. I could talk about it all day. Air, food, water, shelter, seating. In that order. Before money. Before love. Seating. . . . I would remove a display to make space for a chair. I'd rip out a fixture. I'd kill a mannequin. A chair says, 'We care.' Given the chance, people will buy from people who care."
>
> Paco Underhill, *Why We Buy: The Science of Shopping*

Underhill has spent twenty years watching customers in stores, malls, and banks. If he thinks seating is that important, you should, too. If you don't know how much seating you need, invite feedback from someone over seventy, the parents of small children, someone with a mobility impairment, and someone with a fatiguing illness like MS. They'll tell you in a flash where you need to put places to rest. Choose benches with backrests. Indoor benches should have padding or cushions. And make sure you try out seating "in person"; a catalog can't tell you if something is comfortable or not.

Try it before you buy it. Don't defer to an architect or a designer when you're picking out your furniture. And when you're working with a designer, look for someone who is familiar with user-experience design. This will tell you that they have the end user in mind—namely, your visitor. Unfortunately, some designers choose looks over comfort. An expensive new student center at an urban college suffers from this kind of designeritis. The designer chose limited-edition armless chairs shaped like giant squiggles. In the brochure photos, the chairs look like a cool idea. They can be also be used as tables (when laid on their sides), are inexpensive, and are easily cleaned. But the hard plastic isn't comfortable to sit on. The shape means you have to perch on them rather than relax into them, and as a result students avoid the space that was intended expressly for them to use.

An architect or designer isn't with your visitors every day. You are. So make sure you are working with someone who cares about your visitor experience.

Restrooms

The only thing that's worse than being tired is not being able to find a restroom when you need one. Hopefully your new and improved wayfinding (Chapter 9) will help visitors find your restrooms easily. Cleaning, stocking, and maintenance should be your highest priority for your restrooms. I've visited some very nice restaurants with shockingly poor facilities. If you use a staff-only restroom, make sure you examine your visitor restrooms at least once a month. One restaurant owner in Rockport, Massachusetts, had not been inside her own women's room in several years and was horrified to see how grungy it had become despite regular cleaning.

Your brand is reflected in every aspect of your experience. Even if you can't afford high-end fixtures and tile, you can still create a lovely restroom. Paint, especially faux finishing, is an inexpensive way to keep a restroom looking fresh. Lighter colors need less maintenance and fewer touch-ups than dark shades. Make sure you use a washable paint to aid in cleaning. If you sell lotion and soap, use testers in your restrooms to help promote the products. If you don't sell these products, but a nearby store does, why not have the store provide products for your restroom along with a nice little sign promoting their shop?[5] This idea is especially relevant for nonprofit sites with limited budgets. Perhaps a bath and body shop would "sponsor" your restrooms on an annual basis, providing you with quality products and creating a unique restroom experience, while reaping the social capital of collaborating with you.

Common sense should also come into play when you consider your restrooms. If you serve families, provide changing tables in both the men's and women's rooms. If you're building a new family restroom, have one sink placed at child's height to make life easier. Children are afraid of auto-flush toilets, so avoid using those if you can.[6] At Jungle Roots Children's Dentistry in Chandler, Arizona, the unisex restroom also has a diaper pail and a step stool for kids. When you're planning your restroom design, put yourself in your visitors' shoes, and ask for their feedback. Using surfaces like black rubber, aluminum, and tile floors helps cut down on maintenance. Grout must be cleaned and sealed regularly to prevent odors.[7] Make sure every door latches properly and that every stall has a usable hook.

Even if you aren't currently hosting many people with mobility impairments, you soon will be. The Baby Boomers are getting older and will be everywhere in the U.S., demanding better services and accessibility as they age. Whatever the future brings, there's a mom at your front desk right now complaining about how hard it is to get into your restroom with her double stroller. That's why you should consider universal design whenever you are renovating a space or building a new one. Universal design goes beyond ADA accessibility to create solutions that are good for everyone. Consider self-opening doors, restroom entryways with no doors at all (like those in airports), and water fountains and sinks placed at several heights. Sturdy railings are important for helping older visitors feel secure on stairways.[8]

Food

Offering food can increase a visitor's comfort and so her stay time, which frequently leads to additional purchases. If you are more interested in visitors' attention than you are their wallets, remember that offering food also extends museum visits and helps people focus on your educational offerings.[9]

The big three in food service: space, partnering, and theme. You may not have the physical space to provide a restaurant or café, but there may be one nearby. In that case, you could use cross-promotion. Encourage your visitors to use the café, and arrange with the café to display information about your site. If you have limited space, you still might have enough room and traffic for a coffee cart. Rely on experts to run your food-service operation; contract with a vendor to provide beverages and light snacks for a percentage of their income. That's how catering is done in most museums. And museum restaurants and special-events catering can provide a hefty income stream, helping to offset other costs like maintenance or office staff that aren't easy to underwrite.

The best food concessions are themed to a site's offerings; it could be French food during an Impressionist-painting exhibition, tea or sushi at a Japanese garden, or smoothies and energy bars in a park-service visitor center. If you appeal to a family audience, make sure you have some appropriate kid-friendly offerings on your menu.

Very good eateries at nonprofit sites sometimes become destinations in themselves, drawing new visitors who might not come to the site otherwise. To involve those visitors in more of your offerings, use table tents in your restaurant to advertise merchandise, exhibitions, or programs. Promote the restaurant in your publications and advertising. One creative program at the Virginia Museum of Fine Arts in Richmond is "Got Munch?" It includes a fifteen-minute museum tour plus a ten-percent discount on lunch.[10]

Mind comfort

Once their basic physical needs are met, your visitors are willing to pay attention to what you have to offer. This is where another behavioral psychology theory comes into play.

Effort and reward, a delicate balance. Researcher B.F. Skinner found that people are motivated by the greatest reward provided for the least amount of effort.[11] A densely packed sign full of long paragraphs of college-level text doesn't provide enough "reward" to warrant all the work involved in reading it. That's why signs should be easy to read, with large type and lots of empty space in the layout. We'll talk more about signs in the next chapter.

Reward and effort also relate to your Web site and any interactive touch screens you provide. If these look too complicated to use, people will give up or ask a staff person for help. If you bought the touch screens to reduce the burden of questions on staff members, you just wasted a lot of money.

Educational signs follow the same principles. If a sign uses a large typeface, has dark letters on a white background, and has a generous amount of white space in the layout, it creates an impression that the information is easy to access. These physical attributes of the layout provide mind comfort as well. They help a visitor feel smart enough to figure something out instead of feeling threatened or too challenged. Aspects of mind comfort are just as important as body comfort. We talked about orientation in the last chapter, because feeling lost is scary, and scary is uncomfortable. Here are some other aspects of mind comfort for you to consider.

Safety

The second level of Abraham Maslow's pyramid, just above food and shelter, is safety.[12] The same environment might feel very safe to one person and yet scary to another. If you're used to the congestion of a big city, walking on a deserted beach trail might feel scary. (Where are all the people? Is someone following me?) If you're comfortable out in the wilderness, an urban environment full of people invading your space can feel threatening. People get comfortable with new environments through repeated visits, venturing a little farther into new territory each time.[13] Someone who has never been to a museum might not feel comfortable on the first or even the second visit, while a person who grew up visiting museums finds herself at home there.

All kids all the time? It's especially important to create a safe environment for children if you appeal to the family market. This means childproofing, eliminating sharp corners, and providing gates with latches for toddler areas. I've seen people put toddlers in dangerous places (like dangling them over a fence for a better look at a bear) because the design of the area wasn't suited to kids' needs; the child couldn't see over the fence or plantings. And make it clear to parents that they can't drop kids off and leave them unsupervised at your facility unless you have the staffing, insurance, and compliance with safety regulations to provide that service.

Clean and shiny

Mind comfort is also created by places that are well maintained. The broken-window theory states that you must fix the first window that gets broken immediately. Otherwise people will assume that no one cares about the place and it's okay to break more windows. This will lead to more vandalism, and then crime.

Facilities that appear well maintained are less subject to vandalism.[14] The high crime rate that defined New York City in the early 1980s was addressed at first by cleaning the graffiti off the subway cars. Small, seemingly insignificant cases of turnstile jumping and other minor subway crimes were taken very seriously. Over a few years' time that dangerous subway system became a much different place because the authorities paid close attention to maintenance and small-scale crime.

Keeping your site very clean will help shape visitors' behavior if they aren't treating your facilities well or are not spending as much time as you'd like.[15] A clean, well-maintained site tells your visitors that you care. One job for teen staffers at the Seattle Public Library is washing the book jackets and computer keyboards.[16]

If you build it, keep it up. Make sure you don't build something that you can't afford to maintain. This can happen with renovations or new buildings if your architect or designer doesn't key into the realities of your organization. Museums sometimes get into financial trouble a year or two after opening, when attendance doesn't pay for expensive new buildings.

Include money in your annual budget for maintenance, regular cleaning, and the replacing of worn or broken items. Keep an eye on your restrooms and buy good-quality fixtures that will hold up well. You might save a few dollars on a sink when it's installed but if it promptly cracks or begins to drip, you will pay plumbers more than you saved. Green building techniques can cost somewhat more up front but pay for themselves with savings on utilities and water down the line. And your eco-consciousness would be a great selling point for drawing like-minded visitors and creating positive press. In water-starved Southern California, the San Diego Zoo is saving money by installing no-flush urinals; each saves forty thousand gallons of water a year.[17]

Comfort supports learning

Getting physical. In their book *Learning from Museums*, researchers John Falk and Lynn Dierking describe three aspects of learning environments. The first is the physical aspect. (I'll cover the other aspects—intellectual and sociocultural—in the next two chapters.) Learning is completely tied to the environment where it happens, and people can't focus on learning when they're tired or hungry. When you meet the basic physical needs of your visitor, you support their ability to learn. Good memories as well as learning come from good experiences.[18] And good experiences start with a comfortable environment.

Trends in comfort

A site can also offer the comfort of "quiet fascination." Places with that quality allow people to reflect, relax, and recharge. Sometimes just creating a small space within a larger space can create a wonderful retreat where people can rest and be charmed.[19] That's the appeal of small rooms within English walled gardens, miniatures, dollhouses, tree houses, and forts. I've seen mentions of personal refuges and luxury tree houses in several magazines, and there are many books about these tiny, comfortable retreats.[20] If your site is a large, busy place, try using seating, walls, or temporary dividers to create small nooks that allow people sanctuary and privacy. And if your site is likely to attract new mothers, try to offer a private space for nursing.

People also feel most comfortable if they can see ahead but feel supported from behind. Provide your visitors a feeling of "prospect and refuge" by placing a solid shrub or a wall in back of a bench.[21]

The search for safety and sanctuary. In 2005 leading trend spotter Faith Popcorn predicted "nouveau simplicity, control, and comfort" as top trends. Popcorn notes that consumers are spending more time cocooned at home, exhausted from the stresses of work, war, and terrorism.[22] Another trend-watching site listed increased anxiety, the need for authenticity, and the search for happiness as recent top trends.[23] How are companies responding? The 2007 Toyota Camry features an "immune system" that cleans the air of germs, dust, pollen, and mold, plus a new seat fabric that is comfortable in extreme temperatures and on long drives.[24] Restaurant menus that focus solely on comfort foods, like cereal, grilled cheese, or peanut butter are popping up, along with places offering S'mores you can make at your table.[25] Keep your eyes open for trends that apply to your organization's niche, and focus on creating all the mind and body comforts you can for your visitors. Given the trend to cocoon, your challenge is even greater: to lure visitors out by creating a destination with the comforts of home.

Once you have successfully created a comfortable, welcoming environment, what then? Now your visitors are primed and ready to receive your educational content, play with your exhibits, appreciate the esthetics of your offerings, and connect with your collections. They're ready for your communication.

CHAPTER 11

Craft your words carefully

Step #5: Communication
Everything you convey in written or spoken words is included in the communication step.

The goal of the communication step is for every visitor to understand exactly what you mean at all times. When you greet people in person or by telephone, offer assistance, create fun interactions, or provide written information, you're communicating. It's a critical step in creating a memorable visitor experience, and it represents the intellectual context for learning. The way to get people involved and engaged in your organization and connecting with your content is to communicate in a way that's personally relevant, so they can see themselves reflected in what you do.[1]

This chapter starts with the idea of creating a theme for your site, allowing you to coordinate all your communication efforts.[2] We'll then cover how to develop guidelines for both written and verbal communications so you can interact with your visitors and make them part of the experience.

Creating a theme

Before Disneyland, amusement parks and carnivals were a collection of rides, cheap games, and sleazy sideshow attractions along with buckets o' fries. Then Walt Disney invented the *theme* park. Disney adapted the storytelling process from his successful animation studios. He used the unique process of storyboarding when he began developing themed attractions. Disney "imagineers" still create a theme and make storyboards for every new area or ride. Every queue, paint color, and component of the experience carries the message of that theme. For example, at Disney's Animal Kingdom in Florida the snack cart in the Southeast Asia section is made from a real, vividly colored bus imported from India. At a Disney park "everything speaks."[3]

Creating an organizational theme harnesses the power of stories to coordinate your communication. Here's an example. Let's imagine that a newly opened living-history farm wants to develop an organizational theme. They have come up with three possibilities:

- ABC Homestead Museum celebrates the fruits of the earth.
- Families bond through farm life.
- Self-sufficiency is a tradition essential to American life.

How do they decide which theme to use? Each choice is different and conjures up its own mental picture of what their visitor center might look like. "Fruits of the earth" could include a cornucopia, lush images of freshly picked fruits and vegetables, and a harvest color scheme. "Farm life" suggests warmth, Norman Rockwell images, Thanksgiving, and family harmony. "Self-sufficiency" might include a red, white, and blue color scheme and images of victory gardens from World War II.

A good theme helps guide the design of your exterior, interior, signs, printed materials, and Web site. It gives you a framework for shaping the content of your communication with your visitors.

A theme is a big idea—in three parts

How do you develop a good theme? Create one that flows naturally out of your organization's mission and personality, one that will appeal to your target visitors. An organizational theme works in tandem with your mission statement. Great themes include a universal concept like love, family, loyalty, or redemption.[4] At Gettysburg National Military Park in Pennsylvania all the communication revolves around the theme of heroic death and brave sacrifice.[5] You can use museum researcher Beverly Serrell's "Big Idea" process to create a theme for your organization.[6] A theme is simply a sentence made of three parts: 1) a subject, 2) an action verb, and 3) an outcome.

- **1. Subject:** The subject of your theme could be what your organization collects or the name of your organization. But it's stronger if it focuses on something about your visitors, because that makes the theme personally relevant. Avoid using "we" or "our visitors" as a subject; that would make your theme too vague. In the themes I listed for ABC Homestead Museum, above, the subjects are:
  - ABC Homestead Museum—the site's name
  - Families—who could be the target visitors
  - Self-sufficiency—an abstract concept that's historically an American ideal

So, although all three subjects suggest a design direction for the site, only the second—families—is visitor focused. Now let's look at the verb.

- **2. Verb:** Try to avoid using vague or passive verbs like "is," "are," "transforms," "impacts," or "represents." Passive verbs like these don't give forward motion to your theme. Action verbs like "celebrate" and "create" add life and motion to your theme. In the ABC Homestead Museum examples, the verbs are:
  - celebrates
  - bond
  - is

The first two are active verbs, which is good.

- **3. Outcome:** This is the "So what?" for your visitors; it's the answer to the question "Why should I care?" In these examples, the outcome is:
  - the fruits of the earth
  - family togetherness through farm life
  - an American tradition

The second and third are the strongest outcomes in terms of personal relevance to American visitors, but "family togetherness" is the only one that's also a universal theme. So "Families bond through farm life" is the strongest of these three choices for ABC Homestead Museum. It contains personal relevance to the visitor, an action verb, a clear design direction, and a universal concept.

Communicating your theme

Your actual theme statement is for staff use. It's not communicated word for word to your visitors. Instead, you can turn a theme statement into a tag line for the public, something catchy that could be painted on the wall or put on a flyer. Put your new organizational theme to work in all your written communications—signs, flyers, annual reports, and brochures.

Disney's service theme is "We create happiness by providing the finest in entertainment for people of all ages, everywhere."[7] Their public tag line is far simpler: "The Happiest Place on Earth." If the ABC Homestead Museum had "Families bond through farm life" as its theme, its public tag line might be "Celebrate togetherness: ABC Homestead Museum."

Written communication

You have lingo that is unique to your organization: "labels," "interactives," and "signage," are three examples of terms I use in this book that are insider-speak. Make sure that you're not confusing your visitors unnecessarily by throwing in an *oeuf* where an "egg" would do. The more connections you make to visitors' existing knowledge, the better they will understand you. The Carnegie Library in Pittsburgh now calls its reference desk "Ask a Librarian," and the Seattle Public Library changed its circulation desk to "Checkout."[8] If you are translating information into another language, be sure that a native speaker of the language in question checks the meaning for you. At the Borobudur Temple in Java, Indonesia, a sign at the bag check reads "Free of charge for your entrusting bags." Huh?

Tone and voice

As part of your Experience*ology* binder (described on page 139), put together a style manual to guide the people who create your written communication. First, set a tone—so that everything you write sounds consistent. Tone can be thought of as the voice of the person who is speaking through the writing, whether that's a specific person or the voice of your organization.[9]

Rockfish Seafood Grill restaurants, which are decorated to look like fly-fishing lodges, have a tone that is lighthearted and fun, reflecting the sense of humor of the founder, Randy DeWitt. The signs for the restrooms read "2-P." The women's restroom has a 50s-style cartoon painted on a wooden sign: "Inboards." Of course, the men's room has a matching sign: "Outboards." The servers' T-shirts have slogans on the back like "May the fish be with you."[10] The restaurant's tone is communicated consistently through the menus and the in-store signs.

One way to define your tone is by developing a fictional character to represent your organization, or to imagine that you are casting a spokesperson for a commercial. If the character were speaking, what kind of words would he use? How animated would he be? Would he seem formal and stiff, or friendly and approachable? Is the voice of your site a woman's or a man's? This character can be developed to appear in your advertising. A character or spokesperson for a holocaust memorial would use a completely different tone, language, and clothing from one for a children's museum. Some examples of characters used by for-profit businesses are Mickey Mouse, Ronald McDonald, and the Pillsbury Doughboy.

Signs

If you are writing signs of any number or length, set a grade level and readability score as part of your guidelines. The spelling and grammar function of most word processors will allow you to calculate the grade level of highlighted copy and produce a readability score. Writing at a fourth- to sixth-grade level with sixty-percent-plus readability is a good place to begin.[11]

Your sign guidelines should indicate the maximum length in words and the minimum font size that can be used.[12] Choose one serif typeface—like the one you're reading now—for running text and a bold, contrasting **sans-serif** typeface for headlines.[13] (Serifs are the short lines that come out from the edges of some letters. A good example is the capital "L." The chapter titles of this book are in sans-serif type.) And remember that older eyes need strong color contrast. Older readers see everything as being a bit more yellow than it is, and they need more light for reading.[14] I recently saw a magazine article in silver text on white paper! I'm not sure even a twenty-year-old could have read it.

Informational signs. Research supports the idea that informational signs should be no longer than a hundred fifty words, broken up

Older readers see everything as being a bit more yellow than it is, and they need more light for reading.

into three fifty-word paragraphs.[15] Make every word count on an informational sign; I like to think of interpretive signs as educational haiku. If information doesn't fit in the running text, sneak it into the captions for images. Include photos or illustrations to replace words where you can, because pictures help with memory.[16] Use action verbs and tighten up your writing.[17]

Your headlines should tell the story. Use short titles for each paragraph. Test them all to make sure that they tell the story on their own because many visitors won't read the actual text.[18] People use the headlines to decide whether they want to read the paragraph, and they tend to read about a third of what is offered, in a random order.[19] That's why having every component or sign relate to one central theme is so important. Another idea: consider writing a kids' storyline and placing it at their eye level, so they can follow along. And test lifesize mockups of signs in place to make sure they are legible and clearly communicate their messages to visitors.

Effort vs. reward revisited. We talked about these in Chapter 10. The most interesting information might be skipped over if it's presented poorly. It's easier to read signs and brochures when the text uses both upper- and lowercase letters—not all caps—and is flushed left with the right edge left ragged. When reading, people recognize words by their unique shapes, also called their "coastlines." USING ALL CAPS OBLITERATES THE COASTLINE, making all the words look like rectangles.[20] It also looks like you're shouting at people.

Each sign should convey a maximum of five concepts; three is ideal.[21] Grouping the information into three to five concepts allows a reader to make sense of it, and making those concepts tell a story improves people's ability to remember it.[22] If you are writing signs that communicate rules, give the reason for the rule on the sign. People are more likely to comply when reasons are given.[23]

Going bilingual

In the U.S., "bilingual" refers to English plus Spanish. (The following discussion applies, whatever your principal language.) Because it is likely that you have visitors who don't read or speak English, you must decide how to communicate with them. Look to your mission to guide you as you decide how to handle multiple languages. If, for example, you are fully committed to serving the Spanish-speaking audience, then you should print all your signs (or many of them) in both English and Spanish.[24] If you have the occasional visitor who doesn't speak English and your primary goal is to get them from point A to point B, then you might concentrate on maps that use symbols and icons in addition to English. If your site draws an international audience, survey your visitors to find out the top five or ten languages and provide some materials (maps, brochures, flyers) in each language. It's expensive to produce materials in other languages, so never assume you know what the most common languages are. Always do a survey.

Clearly, consistently, internationally. It's difficult to provide direct translation in two or more languages, since blocks of text will be longer in most other languages than in English. Instead, aim for clear information and consistent presentation. Find a qualified writer skilled in the language in question. You are looking for the skills common to advertising copywriting, not just straight translation. Use color and typeface to set off each language, creating visual cues for readers. Be prepared for criticism. Language is a touchy subject and *someone* will probably object to whatever you've done.[25]

Spoken Communication

One summer I worked as a receptionist and had to answer every call with "Towers, Perrin, Forster, and Crosby, good morning. How can I help you?" (If you give your employees a mouthful like that, you make your visitor wait just a little longer to get help.) The people who gave me that telephone script had never repeated it endlessly all day long. Don't force your employees to say something silly or difficult. It's not a job that puts people first, and it's not a job someone will want to excel at or keep for long.

While I don't advocate requiring employees to follow a script, in some cases you'll want to do some intensive training. High school- or college-age employees, regardless of their education or background, need coaching in proper telephone protocol and courtesy-desk etiquette, and they should start out with a script for a set period of time.[26] When they are ready to depart from the script, celebrate that accomplishment. Coach employees about being "onstage" whenever they are with the public. Onstage means no swearing, no discussing their personal lives, and no personal phone calls within earshot of visitors. How many times have you overheard employees complaining about their boss or their boyfriend in the next aisle—or worse still—waited for someone to finish a personal phone call before he rang up your purchase?

If you are using employees or volunteers to give visitors educational information, train them in techniques for engaging the visitors.[27] Choose wisely for positions like this, whether the people doing the job are paid or unpaid. You want people with a natural aptitude for sales, both to persuade and to generate excitement about the topic.[28] Setting down guidelines in your style manual about the theme, tone, and organizational personality you want to transmit will help your employees become a living, active part of your communication step. Staff and volunteers who convey educational information at your site should receive interpretive training in order to learn the guidelines for communication.

A true Experience*ology* organization always looks for ways to shift its offerings in response to visitors' wants and needs. The exercises on pages 179–80 will help you get started on the path to better communication. In the next chapter we'll look at ways to build in engagement, using all five senses to heighten the experience.

Fun and the five senses

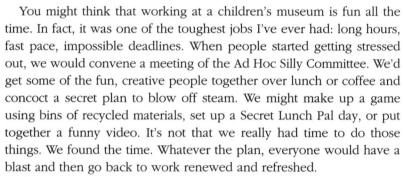

Step #6: Sensation

When you're designing your experience or setting up visitors' interaction with staff, always remember to ask, "Is it fun?" "Does it engage all five senses?" and "Is it unexpected?"

You might think that working at a children's museum is fun all the time. In fact, it was one of the toughest jobs I've ever had: long hours, fast pace, impossible deadlines. When people started getting stressed out, we would convene a meeting of the Ad Hoc Silly Committee. We'd get some of the fun, creative people together over lunch or coffee and concoct a secret plan to blow off steam. We might make up a game using bins of recycled materials, set up a Secret Lunch Pal day, or put together a funny video. It's not that we really had time to do those things. We found the time. Whatever the plan, everyone would have a blast and then go back to work renewed and refreshed.

There's a myth that if people have time to goof off, they aren't going to work hard. But the opposite is true for high-powered, successful companies like IDEO, America's top design firm. The IDEO staff works hard and plays hard, and the company's work environment allows for fun and interaction.[1] Southwest Airlines, the most successful airline in the U.S., also has legendary annual staff parties.[2] Play is a basic human need, as important to our well-being as sleeping and dreaming. It's also critical to dealing with stress. Our need for play, even as adults, is one reason Las Vegas is so successful.[3] Las Vegas-style fun is not appropriate for every work environment, but there are many ways you can bring fun and play into your organization with a tone that fits your brand image.

Fun recharges us. Not only does your staff need to be having fun as a regular part of their day, but so do your visitors. Creating a fun environment refreshes your visitors and makes them want to come back. If you work at a site with somber subject matter like the holocaust, it might not be appropriate to be "fun." Yet a serious tone in the workplace is even more reason your staff needs to lighten up in private. Your visitors will also need respite from the gravity of your subject matter, and you can design that into the experience. I'm not suggesting Groucho glasses for everyone, but see how many of the techniques in this chapter you can incorporate to enrich your experience and make it as enjoyable and engaging as possible.

Humans are social animals

There's a serious reason for investing in fun—it represents the third context for learning, called "sociocultural" by researchers John Falk and Lynn Dierking.[4] (The other two contexts, physical and intellectual, were covered in Chapters 10 and 11.) While some people do visit sites alone, many come with groups of family or friends.

Consider how you can foster social interaction by creating spaces that encourage conversation and group activities.[5] Design spaces or activities to be used by more than one person at a time and by people of all ages.[6] Back in the early 90s the Chicago Academy of Sciences had an exhibition about decreasing our use of global resources. One popular station was a computer interactive that allowed you to calculate the size of your family's "footprint" on the earth by answering a series of questions. The computer attracted kids, who would sit down and start playing with it. But they soon had to call over a parent to answer questions such as "How many miles do you drive per year?" Every day the staff would find two stools in front of the computer, even though there was supposed to be only one. The parents were dragging another stool over to the station to work with their children. Think about designing interactives that need at least two people to complete them; or create enough space around some installations to allow friends to use them together.[7]

At the Tables of Content restaurant in Newport, Oregon, diners are seated at tables of eight and served family style. The server invites them to play a game. Each person is asked to tell the table "two truths and a lie," and the other diners try to guess the lie by asking questions. You might use this technique as an icebreaker during a tour or special event. Near Salzburg, Austria, you can take a tour of a salt mine. At different points during the tour you pair up with another person, since you need a partner to help you slide down from level to level in the dark.[8]

If experiences are too rigidly designed, they lack the elements of discovery and play. Avoid being too predictable, like giving visitors one entrance and one exit in an exhibition space, for example. And go easy on exhibits with predetermined outcomes, like buttons you push to make things light up. Instead, think of how you can provide a variety of choices and options. Let visitors decide the outcome in some installations. Think of ways you can reward visitors for interacting with each other, as it will increase their enjoyment and learning.[9] At the Brookfield Zoo in Illinois, there is a huge outdoor game that teaches school groups about consumer choices that are good for the environment. You can't play the game alone; it takes a group of people cooperating to move through it. If you need more ideas, all the group challenges on the popular TV show *Survivor* are designed as cooperative games. This type of global group play is the basis for many interactive Web sites like flickr.com, kooltag.com, yellowarrow.net, and grafedia.net.

Five-sense synergy

We frequently offer experiences that focus on just one or two senses. It's the rare experience that engages all five. It might not be easy to add stimuli for all the senses to your experience, but this chapter will give you ideas that can round out what you offer. Visitors who have had a complete sensory experience remember it and tend to rate it highly.[10] Your staff members can create memorable sensory experiences through their special skills; there's a "cup flipper" at the Casa de Fruta Restaurant in Hollister, California, and an amazingly expert sheep shearer at Gledswood Homestead and Winery in Catherine Fields, NSW, Australia. These extraordinary features make those sites unforgettable.

At an art gallery or museum, you can add music to enhance the visuals you offer. But visitors can't touch, taste, or smell the art. To enrich the experience, you could add a branded scent to your gallery's HVAC system, offer people tastes of foods themed to the art, and provide texture samples that mimic the feel of the artworks on view.

If you have a restaurant concession, your visitors are focused on taste. Before the food is brought to the table, consider giving customers some fun visual stimuli to fill their wait time. Local artists can display their works in your food-service space. Or you can add unusual-textured napkin rings for people to feel. You can play music, or open the kitchen door so visitors can hear the sizzle of the grill. Let them smell the seasonings of their meal.

If you can, create full-body experiences instead of just the passive— and more common—experiences of sitting, standing, or reading. Can you have people crawl, lean, lie down, or dance as part of your experience? At the Carnegie Library in Pittsburgh, the Teen Space offers a "Dance, Dance Revolution" contest every Friday afternoon.[11] If you sell electrical appliances or games in your shop, plug them in so that visitors can hear the noises they make, see them in action, and play with them. People want to know how a game works, view a CD-ROM, and sniff a candle or potpourri.[12]

If you sell clothing, think of your dressing rooms as selling spaces. Make sure they are kept clean, that the lighting is good, that there's enough room, and that there are plenty of hooks. Many department stores have tiny dressing rooms with cruel lighting, worn carpet, missing hardware, scuffed laminate, and piles of pins and other trash. Not only does that reflect poorly on the store's brand, but most decisions about whether to buy clothing are made in the dressing room! Encourage your visitors to feel good about your products by offering them a dressing room that creates positive emotions.

Broaden your vision

Seventy percent of your body's sense receptors are in your eyes.[13] Make the most of the sense of sight through creative lighting, color, contrast, and movement. The Brooklyn Children's Museum had a memorable exhibition called *The Mystery of Things*. Spotlights with cutouts (called "gobos")[14] were used in the entry hallway to throw question-mark-shaped shadows on the floor, an inexpensive way to introduce the theme.

The sense of sight strongly affects sales. A bottle of wine with a picture of an animal on the label outsells others by two to one.[15] People like to see condensation on containers of bottled water or soda or they don't believe they're cold.[16] In taste-test research, the color of the product or the shade of the color on the label can override the perception of taste. People believe orange-flavored soda is actually cherry if it's colored red, and they think that 7-Up tastes more lemony or limey depending on the amount of yellow or green used on the label.[17] A children's museum could offer tastes of the green eggs and ham—first cooked up by Dr. Seuss—and use the experience to talk about perception.

Excite the eyes. Create visual appeal by using extremes—things that are very large or very small and very colorful. Sometimes the emotional impact comes from volume. At the United States Holocaust Memorial Museum in Washington, D.C., one of the most powerful sights is the piles and piles of the victims' empty shoes. You can introduce unexpected contrast by providing novel and surprising things in unexpected combinations.[18] And when you design experiences, don't forget to consider *all* the views a visitor might have. The view into the storeroom, the restroom, and the kitchen should either be designed to be seen or blocked off from view.[19]

Singapore Airlines might be the company that's done the ultimate in visual branding by creating the "Singapore Girl" in 1973. To be a flight attendant for the airline at that time, women had to be younger than twenty-six and had to fit into a petite single-size uniform made from high-quality silk. The women could pick one of two color combinations for their outfits, which matched the decor in the cabins. They had to be beautiful enough to model for an ad and were specially trained in how to move and talk to passengers.[20]

Those rigid standards wouldn't hold up under today's U.S. employment law, but they demonstrate how visual branding can be continued throughout an organization. Make sure you have visual consistency throughout your site, your Web site, your uniforms, and the printed materials you publish. Create your own branded images and work with one designer or design team to craft your branded look.

What does your brand sound like?

Nothing transports you through time faster than hearing an old song. Suddenly you're back in the school gym dancing with that senior who seemed so cool or with your first love. In Chapter 8, I mentioned the front porch chimes at the Lost Whale Bed & Breakfast in Trinidad, California. The proprietors could incorporate that custom-made sound into their brand by adding it to their Web site and mixing it into a soundtrack that's played in the rooms. They could also sell sets of "Lost Whale" chimes to interested guests. The brand would then surely travel by word of mouth when the people who bought the chimes were asked about them. If you manage a garden, park, or nature center, you could incorporate this idea as well.

Sound is even important to brands that might not seem to focus on sound. Kellogg's has not only trademarked the "snap, crackle, pop" of their Rice Crispies, they have patented the *crunch* of their cornflakes. Daimler-Chrysler has an entire division dedicated to designing the satisfying sound of their car doors. These companies understand the power of sound to both create and enhance an impression of unique quality.[21]

You can enhance your experience by adding music or an ambient soundscape or by installing sound effects activated by motion sensors in your space. If you have eating or shopping at your site, music helps relax people, increasing the likelihood of their buying. (People spend more when classical music is playing.) If you want to speed the lunch crowd up at your food-service concession, play music with a brisk tempo and leave your tables bare. To slow people down at dinner, play slower music and use tablecloths. These techniques also seem to increase the bar bill and encourage spending on coffee and dessert.[22]

In learning environments, complex music seems to interfere with comprehension, but it improves people's performance on nonverbal tasks.[23] So if you want people to read, don't play music; however, if people are solving spatial puzzles, music can enhance the experience. If you are having trouble with crime or graffiti in public areas, try playing classical music over a loudspeaker system. It's working in Australia, Denmark, and the Port Authority bus terminal in New York.[24]

There are new audio speakers on the market that can target sound into a precise listening area with no bleedthrough, so that people standing or sitting in one area can hear sounds that are inaudible just a few feet away.[25] With these tools, you can use sound to add a sophisticated edge to your site and set you apart from your competition.

Creating a taste for your brand

It's important to come up with imaginative ways to include tastes, especially if you don't offer food. We have ten thousand taste buds in our mouths, all ready for an impression.[26] I once designed a garden tour called "Incredible Edibles." During the walk participants were introduced to the six parts of a plant and shown edible examples of each. Along the way people got a little sample of jicama root, sugar cane stems, mint leaves, nasturtium flowers, and chocolate-covered espresso beans (the fruit of the coffee tree). We finished up with popcorn (seeds). People didn't expect to taste things during a garden tour, and the experience made the information from the tour guide come alive.

The power of the taste buds is harnessed when a cookie shop in a mall offers you a nibble; the same power accounts for the way you can have "lunch" by touring the sample carts in a grocery store. People like to taste a food before they buy it. Retail researcher Paco Underhill believes ninety percent of all new grocery products fail because companies don't include sampling as part of their introduction and marketing plans.[27] Many museum shops offer packaged food items and could enhance their sales by offering tastes during busy periods.

Offer tiny samples of food you sell or food that matches the theme of your organization. At the San Diego Museum of Man, a woman makes tortillas by hand several days a week in the Maya exhibit. You can watch her work and can buy a fresh, hot tortilla or quesadilla. People who work near the museum sometimes walk over to get quesadillas for lunch, and it's a wonderful surprise for museum visitors to smell the tortilla griddle and to buy an authentic taste on the spot.

The smell of success

Scent may be the most powerful of our five senses because it's the only one that's linked directly to the most ancient part of our brains, the limbic system. The limbic system is also where memory and emotion are stored.[28] We have five million receptors in our noses.[29] Some smells are unique to experiences we have, like the smell of incense at Wat Phrathat Doi Suthep in Chiang Mai, Thailand, or of sulphur at the Artist Paint Pots in Yellowstone National Park in Wyoming.

Pleasant scents have been found to increase visitors' stay time, improve their moods, and enhance learning.[30] Stores use scents to increase sales—a swimwear shop in Sydney, Australia, pumps a coconut smell into the air; a chain of kids' clothing stores in England uses a baby-powder scent. Brewing coffee, baking bread, or grilling chickens in a store sells more of those items. The movie theater experience is indelibly linked to the smell of popcorn. Casinos use scents to increase earnings; slot machines in areas sprayed with a pleasant scent make forty-five percent more in revenue than machines in an "unscented" area.

Casinos use scents to increase earnings; slot machines in areas sprayed with a pleasant scent have been found to make forty-five percent more in revenue than machines in an "unscented" area.

You might assume that new cars smell of plastic and vinyl, but actually new cars don't have much smell. The "new car smell" is sprayed onto the interior before the car leaves the factory floor and disappears in about six weeks. Automobile companies even design unique branded scents to be sprayed into their cars.

Remember the Singapore Girl? In the 1990s Singapore Airlines added a branded scent to their planes, which was also blended into the perfume worn by their flight attendants. It is described as "smooth, exotically Asian, and distinctly feminine."[31]

The JORVIK Viking Centre in York, UK, offers all sorts of scents to heighten the visitor experience—roast beef in the kitchen scene, apples in the market, and fish at harborside—and there's even the odor of a cesspit at the model of an old Viking latrine![32]

How can you add scent to your experience? There are machines available that emit subtle fragrances through the HVAC system into an entire building or within a few feet of an exhibit. Fragrance companies can create a branded scent for you or you can choose one from a company's library. You could also purchase a unit sold for home use with a smaller range of scents.[33] Whether you want to attract visitors, keep them, or enhance their experiences, consider how you might blend scent into your offerings. But do remember to be sensitive to people with allergies.

The power of touch

Our skin is the largest organ in our bodies,[34] yet we seldom take full advantage of this sense in creating memorable experiences. Hershey's Kisses, Toblerone candy bars, and the Volkswagen Beetle all have unique shapes that feel special.[35]

In 1915 designers were asked to create a bottle that could be recognized by touch alone, even in the dark or if it broke into pieces. Brand guru Martin Lindstrom believes that, as Coca-Cola abandons its signature glass bottle—the most famous bottle in the world—they are losing a key element unique to their brand. In the retail world touch is a key factor in decision making. Be sure that your displays are not so neat and tidy that people are afraid to touch them; if they are, they won't buy products from those displays.[36]

To make the most of the need to touch, use unusual textures like fake fur, suede, carpet tiles, or bumpy plastics on walls, seating, displays, and exhibits. Try adding surfaces made from embossed metal, glass block, acoustical egg crate, or the materials normally used on floors for detectable warning systems (for people with visual impairments). Check out construction catalogs to give you ideas, then use those finishes and surfaces in unexpected ways.[37]

If you have objects that can't be touched, can you display something with a similar tactile surface nearby and encourage people to touch it? This would work well in art museums, where an inexpensive porcelain cup might be placed in front of a display of Chinese porcelain, or a rough raku-glazed tile could stand in for an artist's piece. Water is a great way to incorporate touch. Disney uses programmed fountains to get people to splash and play.[38] Stores like Bath and Body Works include a sink for customers to wash their hands in after trying out products. (And that's a good idea for you too if you're offering touchables that must be rinsed off.)

Practical magic

Disney uses that term to describe how it designs repeatable surprises for its guests. While the outcome of a magic trick is not a surprise to the magician, it is to the audience. You know when the surprise is going to occur, but the visitor doesn't.[39]

By its nature, surprise is random and unexpected. Author T. Scott Gross adds that great customer service—out of proportion to the situation—becomes memorable.[40] It's "out of proportion" to lend a customer whose luggage has been lost a suit for an important meeting, but a business develops incredible loyalty when it treats its customers this way.

Here are some ways to create surprises: Instead of advertising discounts, randomly spread out the value of the discount over the year and delight a few visitors with something free. If you offer ticket packages, hit a lucky visitor with an upgrade on occasion. If you offer gifts to premier members or donors, change them every year or customize them based on a person's purchasing habits.[41] Comp a meal for a table, for no reason, to thank customers in your restaurant for their business.

For sites that are more serious in nature, practical magic can still be a part of the plan. Offer visitors a free pass to return or to share with friends. Provide an unscheduled tour with the executive director or board president. Let a select few people touch objects that are normally off limits.

In the next chapter we'll talk about incorporating a variety of common-sense factors into the behind-the-scenes aspects of your organization.

CHAPTER 13

Using your heads

Step #7: Common sense
The common-sense step provides smarter, more logical, more efficient ways to run your business. It includes using visitor studies, applying trends, realigning your mission if necessary, and collaborating with like-minded organizations.

This chapter will help you apply common-sense thinking to your operations. First I'll discuss three key types: operational, cultural, and alignment common sense, a lack of which can fell even the largest companies. We'll talk about soliciting input from your front-line staff members, who can offer you a wealth of money-saving information. Keeping up with cultural trends allows you to shift your business strategy to capitalize on what's happening outside your door. The importance of visitor studies, both formal and informal, is also key to informing your decisions. Visitor-centered organizations use two-way communication, like visitor studies, to fine-tune their offerings. We'll also look at nuts-and-bolts issues like prices and operating hours. Last, we'll cover how to make the most of partnerships large and small, including some you haven't thought of.

Operating on common sense. Every organization has a story to tell about a failure to use common sense. A state park system recently spent $100,000 on a branding study. The specs provided by the branding agency included a color scheme that was impossible for the client's contracted vendor to duplicate and an unusual font that wasn't available in the state computer system. The park system failed to create something with operational common sense.

Got cultural common sense? Sometimes companies fail to use this precious commodity. Control Data Corporation had trouble breaking into the Japanese market in the 1970s. After they'd spent months in fruitless negotiations with ministry officials, someone finally clued them in. The ministers had been too polite to tell them, but the

During a major renovation, my supermarket placed a large TV facing the checkouts at the exit. The TV had a custom-made cabinet that proclaimed "We're redesigning our store to serve you better!" I asked why the set wasn't on and was told that the DVD didn't repeat automatically. Someone restarted it immediately, but I could only watch a few seconds before the checkout line started to back up behind me. (A DVD is only appropriate if customers can see it *while they're waiting in line*, not after they've reached the register.) On subsequent visits I noticed that the set was off, obscured by a new movie display. Eventually it disappeared, brought down by a lack of operational common sense.

translation they were using for "Control Data Corporation" meant "We give gonorrhea" in Japanese.[1] Chevrolet has a legendary screw-up story: they tried to sell the Chevy Nova in Latin America with disastrous results. "No va" means "no go" in Spanish.

Even Disney stumbled. They named their first European theme park—near Paris—EuroDisney, a name that ignored the intense national pride of the French. And EuroDisney didn't serve wine, a beverage central to the French concept of entertainment. Both problems have been addressed, and the park, now called Disneyland Paris, is much more successful.[2] Disney learned an important lesson, and the design of Hong Kong Disneyland incorporates the Chinese concept of feng shui, showing respect for local custom. It even opened on a day considered auspicious in Chinese culture.[3]

Alignment common sense and you. At other times companies fail to use alignment common sense; they don't match their actions with their company's values. Ford Motor Company has invested heavily in green business practices and introduced the first hybrid SUV to the American market. So I was shocked to see a magazine ad for the Ford F-150 pickup. The tailgate of the truck, featured in the ad, has twenty-seven tree stump symbols on it, as if the owner were making notches on his belt every time he cut down a tree. The ad copy reads, "What's your mission?" and later says, "Consider it mission accomplished." My first thought was, here's an ad for a huge, gas-guzzling truck; *I* think their mission is to destroy the environment. Mission accomplished?! I'll bet my impression is not what the company intended when they wrote the ad.

In the UK, Barclays Bank spent millions producing a series of ads featuring Sir Anthony Hopkins as a millionaire banker. The ad campaign, with the slogan "In a big world you need a big bank," had to be pulled almost immediately because it coincided with the closing of many of Barclays' rural branches. Barclays seemed like a snooty global bank that only wanted millionaires as clients.[4]

It's easy to hear one of these stories and shake your head in disbelief. But it's complicated running any business, especially as it grows larger and is harder to oversee. Sometimes problems are due to inertia, or being too close to a subject for too long. In some organizations there's a disconnect between common sense and day-to-day operations. Top businesses and organizations make it a point to constantly ask, "Can we do better?"[5] Strong, healthy organizations welcome critical voices from staff members at every level. This chapter will give you some tools for applying common sense to your organization and avoiding costly mistakes.

Gold mine on the front line

When the MGM Grand Casino in Las Vegas was working to improve its wayfinding signage, managers were somewhat surprised to find that the most valuable information came from the security guards and cocktail waitresses.[6] Think about it. Who else is standing on the floor of the casino interacting with patrons day in and day out? When the City of Seattle was building its flagship public library, they included someone from the security and custodial staff at every design meeting. They've continued this practice for branch building projects as well.[7]

Ask the doorman. Your front-line staff members know more about your visitors than you do. They know how often regulars come, what they do or buy, and what they complain about. They know what questions get asked repeatedly. They'll tell you, if you ask, how to improve day-to-day operations and avoid unnecessary expenses. Make the most of this resource by actively soliciting their input, especially before you roll out new exhibitions, change the layout of your site, or invest in new signage or fixtures. The front-line staff will help you catch problems before they become expensive failures. And new hires, with their fresh points of view, will be able to spot policies or procedures that don't make sense. Commerce Bank in Cherry Hill, New Jersey, increased profits *two thousand percent* in ten years by getting everyone on the staff to think like retailers. Their "Kill a Stupid Rule" program rewards employees with $50 for anything they point out that keeps the bank from wowing its customers.[8]

The brand-new Georgia Aquarium in Atlanta listened to its staff members when their new floors were being poured. They made sure the contractor placed the drain at the lowest point. Staffers knew that at most aquariums large puddles of water must be squeegeed toward the drains all day long.[9]

At my newly renovated grocery store, front-line staff had no input in the remodeling decisions, but they bore the impact of locating products for confused customers, dusting the shelves during construction, rearranging all the merchandise, and restocking shelves frequently. (The new shelves don't hold as much stock as the old ones did.) I'm willing to bet that front-line input could have saved that grocery company a lot of money. Does any of this remind you of a museum expansion project you've been involved in?

Keeping up with trends

Malcolm Gladwell's book *The Tipping Point* does an elegant job of describing how trends can be created or influenced. Keep up with trends that relate to your visitors by following trend-watching Web sites, which are regularly updated. Several of these provide free e-mail newsletters.[10]

For example, two trends in 2005–6 were high-end travel and nostalgia. Luxury tree houses combined both of these, allowing people to camp out in style; there were good mattresses on the beds, down comforters, and gourmet chocolate for the fireside S'mores. A botanical garden or arboretum could take advantage of this trend by offering luxury campouts or old-fashioned games like Capture the Flag, with out-of-the-ordinary snacks afterward. The site's retail shop could package gourmet ingredients, complete with forks and fuel, for making S'mores at home.

Once you are aware of trends, you'll start to see them in magazines, on television, and even in movies. Stay ahead of your competition by keeping an eye on trends and shaping your offerings to reflect them.

Ask the audience

On the TV game show *Who Wants to Be a Millionaire?* a contestant has just one chance to poll the studio audience for help in answering a multiple-choice question. Take every opportunity you have to ask your audience how you are doing and how you can serve them better. There are many ways—both informal and formal—to gather information.

Quick and dirty. You can collect information very effectively by having your staff members ask casual questions while they're working with visitors, then capturing those comments in a notebook or log. Simply watch what visitors do while they're at your site. Paco Underhill's firm, Envirosell, uses a technique called the "density check." Once an hour researchers buzz through, noting on a map where (and how many) customers are in a store.[11] This gives the company a snapshot of activity and indicates under- and overused areas as well.

Another way to track usage is to look for physical evidence of customer activity, including nose- and handprints on glass, worn carpeting, and broken interactive exhibits or touch screens.

One car dealership hired a group of taxi drivers to ferry around customers whose cars were being fixed. The service manager told the drivers to call him immediately if a customer reported any dissatisfaction. People are sometimes more willing to voice complaints to a third party whom they see as disinterested or neutral.[12] If there are cab drivers who regularly drop visitors off at your site, consider asking for their input.

Getting formal. Any information you gather will be useful, but sometimes you need in-depth feedback, which requires formal means. You can use questionnaires or visitor interviews to gather information. Or you might want to put together a focus group if you're developing new programs or exhibitions. These groups give you the time to get into details over an hour or two.

A general manager of the Harvey Hotel in Plano, Texas, used "regulars" to give him detailed feedback. After checking in, these customers would come to the manager's office, where he would give each of them a secret task: to call for room service at 3:00 a.m.; to request fifteen bath towels; or to break a glass in the restaurant. Each assignment came with a feedback sheet, which the guests later returned to the manager. They were rewarded with free meals or one-night passes.[13] The manager used this process to gauge how his staff responded to customers in challenging circumstances. If you feel that your customer-service standards are poor, and you have a large site, try this technique to see where you need to improve.

At big museums, parks, or zoos you can do a tracking study. That means you actually follow one person (or group) over the course of a visit, observing where they go, what they do, and how much time they spend, noting it all on a map of your site.[14]

The power of pictures. You can also videotape visitors—without audio—to see exactly what they're doing. These studies are time- and labor-intensive and are therefore relatively expensive to conduct, but they provide a wealth of detailed, in-depth information. For legal reasons you must inform visitors when you are doing tracking studies and videotaping and assure them that you will not be capturing their conversations. Your disclosure can be made by putting a sign at your entrance or by printing a notice on the back of your tickets. If your site already has security video surveillance, watch an hour or two of tape to see what visitors are doing. (Federal sites have strict guidelines about conducting visitor research, so check those before you begin.)

One new approach to tracking visitors' preferences is to ask them to take pictures of whatever catches their eye or has meaning for them. The images reflect both what people like and dislike during their experience. You can ask them to use their own digital cameras and download the photos before they leave or provide them with Web access in order to upload pictures and comments. This provides you with incredibly detailed information for relatively little cost.[15] Last, search for your site's name once a month on myspace.com, flickr.com, and youtube.com. You'll learn a lot about what visitors are doing without having to ask them a thing.

Use visitors as tiebreakers. There's another reason for asking the audience its opinions: it can help resolve conflicts between experts on your staff and the people who are more in touch with your visitors. Instead of fighting over an issue, test it out with the public. It's much easier to convince certain staff members to shift their thinking when it's not *you* fighting *them*, but information you've gathered from your visitors that's making the point.[16] Web-site-usability expert Cia Romano shows her clients videos of people testing the client's Web site. That allows the client to see and hear exactly what users say as they try to navigate through the site.[17]

The Detroit Institute of Arts is transforming everything about its visitor experience. (They've used Beverly Serrell's "Big Idea" technique, which I discussed in Chapter 11.) After working with consultants like Serrell, weighing input from visitor-feedback groups, and sifting through a decade of visitor studies, they have begun creating one of the first visitor-centered art museums in the U.S. Everything from font size, wall color, and the wording of labels to seating and signage was up for review and major change. Visitors' feedback even led the institute to address cultural issues; when Muslims expressed concerns about nudity in the art, the institute found a way to present works containing nude figures off the beaten path. Four interdepartmental teams are working to bring a balanced view to the planning, with non-art people representing the visitors' perspective. This dramatic overhaul is scheduled for completion in the fall of 2007.[18]

I've used both informal and formal techniques over the years. It's fun and surprising to see what people do and say, and I've learned that my assumptions can be dead wrong. I once surveyed all the educational signs at a zoo to better understand what was currently offered and how to improve it. Along the way I found a very small diagram labeling the various parts of a bird's body. It was in poor condition, at the end of a long row of signs; the typeface was tiny, and it seemed too complicated and obscure to be of much use to visitors. I thought it was a terrible sign, and would have bet $100 that no one had ever read it. But while I was standing there a family walked up. The daughter said excitedly, "Look! Isn't this interesting? Here are all the body parts of a bird!" They proceeded to pore over the sign, pointing out parts of the birds that were hopping around in front of them. I learned that I shouldn't assume I know what every visitor wants. Neither should you. You have to ask them.

The Historic Hudson Valley sites in New York State found some surprises when they surveyed their audience. They assumed that families with children were visiting in large numbers, but it turned out that only one of their six sites had a large family audience. They also assumed that a large number of visitors who came for a special event would return for a regular visit, but they learned that only twenty percent did.[19] The sites are using the information from surveys to develop programs and products that serve their visitors better.

Two-way communication

In the past, most communication between businesses and their customers was one way. In the advertising and marketing world it was known as push communication—the information is pushed out to the consumer who may or may not want it. In pull communication, the customer is actively seeking information about products from companies. But true push-pull communication involves companies shaping their offerings based on consumer input.[20]

New technology to the rescue. One way to get visitors involved in your experience is to encourage them through your Web site or blogs to help shape what you offer.[21] "Blog" is short for "Web log"; it's an easy-to-update Web site that often looks like an online newspaper. Podcasting is another digital tool for communication; it allows anyone to create a personalized audio tour of a museum or similar site. Podcasts can then be shared free on the Internet.[22] Smart sites encourage visitors to create podcasts and then advertise these multiple points of view, renting out MP3 players to people who arrive without them. Organizations might even create brief weekly or monthly podcasts on their Web sites and include a special discount "password" to reward loyal visitors for listening and learning about new exhibitions or classes.

Pricing, products, and hours

When you talk to your visitors, ask them about your services, prices, products, and hours. You may get valuable ideas about new products or programs, or find that you have to shift your prices in some areas. You'll learn what hours of operation will meet demand and still be cost effective. In Chapter 3, I suggested taking advantage of longer seasonal daylight hours or holidays.

A nature center in Minnesota offers nighttime programs like moonlight hikes and astronomy events to specialized audiences like scouts and other organized groups. These pre-booked programs provide revenue without making it necessary to open the entire center, thus saving on staffing.[23]

In response to the growing older demographic in the U.S., many ski resorts in the American West are offering more slopes with fewer moguls and better grooming. One even offers a class called "Bumps for Boomers," which teaches older skiers how to ski moguls with less fatigue and joint stress.[24] If you manage a recreational site, are there ways you can target this older but still active audience in a similar way?

Consider breaking your experience into pieces and charging separate prices for each (such as parking, admission, IMAX, and guided tours). This allows your visitors the flexibility to customize their experiences while you increase your earning power. Alternatively, you might decide it's better to offer somewhat more expensive packages with valuable options bundled together. Just make sure that you aren't pricing yourself out of your market and that you are offering good value for the money you charge.

Ask visitors for feedback about your telephone service and Web site. You can't be open 24/7, but your voice mail and Web site must always be available.[25] Check in with visitors to make sure that these services are easy to use and are improving their perception of your site.

The Burrell Collection in Glasgow, Scotland, got some surprising information from potential visitors when they surveyed the neighborhood. People said that they'd never been to this art museum because the admission was "too expensive." But in fact the admission had always been free! The staff could have assumed that these potential visitors were stupid; instead they learned from their neighbors' responses that their museum *looked like* it was an expensive place to visit. It also must have looked like a place people didn't *want* to visit; otherwise they'd have discovered it was free. The museum used this audience-survey information to create innovative new outreach programs that made the site more relevant to local people's lives.[26]

It can be a little tricky to get at all the details of your audience's responses with surveys; people tend to say that they like what you're doing even if they have some reservations. (And they will always agree that you should have lower prices!) Use the evaluation book in the Further Reading section on page 183 to help you develop effective questions, or consider hiring a consultant who specializes in audience research. Visit www.experienceology.com for up-to-date resources in this area. And be sure to pilot test any change you're considering before you commit to it.

Creating partnerships

Maybe you've already formed good working partnerships with other companies or organizations. Or perhaps you think that partnerships are only for big organizations with large development staffs. Creative partnering can work for any size institution, and it can increase your revenues and enhance your visitor experience.

Find partners whose missions match yours. Start your partnership quest by looking for like-minded organizations. A museum might partner with schools, libraries, and youth organizations to develop programs or exhibitions that appeal to children and teachers. The World Wildlife Fund has been teaching people about the importance of biodiversity by partnering with organizations as varied as the Sierra Club, Disney's Animal Kingdom, and the U.S. Fish and Wildlife Service.[27]

The owners of the South Bark Dog Wash in San Diego decided that it would benefit them to organize the other businesses in their neighborhood, so they started the South Park Business Council. Together they host a quarterly event called the South Park Walkabout. These evening events include free bus rides around the neighborhood and special activities like food, raffles, bingo, and music. The business council also produces a full-page ad in the monthly neighborhood newspaper, creating the sense that South Park is a destination. Pooling their resources has served these small businesses better than running individual ads would have done. Is your site involved in your local business council? If not, consider joining and exploring partnerships in your immediate area.

Art museums in Baltimore and New York are partnering with medical schools. One program broadens students' attitudes toward death and dying by offering them the art of other cultures to study. Another pairs up medical students with senior citizens. This improves the students' attitudes toward geriatric care while offering an improved self-image to the seniors.[28] Cardiologists in Arkansas have teamed up with mayors and a judge to develop the Arkansas River Trail and to promote healthy behaviors like regular exercise.[29]

Partnering well with large companies. Many corporations want to broaden their audiences and/or create goodwill by aligning their businesses with sites like yours. This was how traditional corporate sponsorship worked for hospitals, symphony orchestras, and museums.

The days of large corporate donations are winding down, but corporations still need to create goodwill for their brand by investing in things that their customers care about.[30] They might not be able to donate a lump sum of $50,000, but that doesn't mean they aren't interested in partnering in a new way. Perhaps you can offer classes to their staff members or clients. You might teach financial investors how to build a photography collection, or conduct creativity workshops for a company's executives. In exchange, your corporate partner could lend you marketing, branding, or fundraising talent as part of their volunteer efforts.[31] In Chapter 5, I mentioned that Conservation International, a nonprofit environmental group, is partnering with large corporations like McDonald's to make an impact on the fast-food giant's global supply chain.

In Amsterdam, ING Bank has partnered with the Netherlands National Museum (Rijksmuseum) by providing comfortable couches in the museum's galleries. In Dutch, "bank" is a synonym for "couch," so this clever partnership promotes the ING brand while providing a real benefit to the museum.[32]

Traditional advertising is less and less effective with the glut of daily media messages. Can a partnership with you give a company brand presence with your visitors? Perhaps investing in your site as a destination draws in potential customers and benefits the partner's brand too.[33] The Eastern State Penitentiary historic site in Philadelphia has developed a highly successful haunted-house program. "Terror Behind the Walls," presented each October, nets $500,000 a year. A local radio station provides $25,000 in free advertising. A pizza chain and a costume shop provide coupons at their stores that bring customers to the haunted house. While the program itself is not historically accurate, the money raised has saved the crumbling structure, supporting both historical tours and paying for critical needs like roofing and portable toilets, which are difficult to cover with grants.[34]

Parallel businesses as partners. Organizations about the same size as your site can increase their customer base or offer new products by partnering with you. These businesses might be in a completely different field, and at first you may not seem to have similar goals. But partnering could provide benefits for both of you.

Less than half a mile away from the Quail Botanical Gardens in

Encinitas, California, is a yoga studio. If these two organizations teamed up, the garden could offer yoga classes in its beautiful outdoor setting. The yoga studio would then have a unique product to sell and could target the membership of the garden as well. The garden could reach a number of people who might never have ventured onto the grounds before, becoming a part of their lifestyle during the run of the class. The Munson-Williams-Proctor Arts Institute in Utica, New York, has launched a similar partnership with a local yoga studio, and it's been successful for both organizations.[35]

Taste, a gourmet cheese shop in San Diego, is partnering with O'Brien's Pub to offer classes on pairing beers with cheeses. Taste holds classes both at its shop and the pub, to increase the reach of both. If your museum had an exhibition on Irish art or history, a program like this could bring in an entirely new audience for you.

The Dowse Museum in The Hutt, New Zealand, has successfully partnered with a shopping mall and a hospice. An annual event benefiting the hospice draws car dealers, truck companies, retail shops, and the local police department. Coordinating this event creates goodwill for the museum and brings together partners who might not support the arts directly but want to help the hospice.[36]

Southwest Airlines uses one of its Rapid Rewards mileage partners to provide an employee perk. Southwest's Star Employee of the Month gets a free car for a month, courtesy of Thrifty Car Rental.[37] Offering this type of perk to one of your best employees, or to your members, could be a clever use of a partnership for you as well.

You'll find many examples of creative partnering in the new trend of value-added waiting spaces: hotel lobbies offering free WiFi and Internet access courtesy of Yahoo!; free supermarket concerts in the Netherlands sponsored by Dommelsch Beer; lounges at Amsterdam's Schiphol Airport offering meeting space, online access, food, and beverages for customers of ABN AMRO Bank; or the LG Wash Bar in Paris, where customers can have a drink while they do their laundry and try out various LG brand machines.[38] Use these ideas to expand your concept of what partnering could look like for your site. The exercises begin on page 184.

You have a wealth of common sense available to you when you put all your staff members to work creating smarter ways of doing business. Use these common-sense techniques to your best advantage by getting regular feedback from your front-line employees, keeping up with trends, asking your visitors what they want, and creating smart partnerships that increase the power and alignment of your business.

As the eight-step process draws to a close, it's time to consider your finale. How are you ending your visitor's experience? Have you given as much thought to the last impression you make as you gave to your first?

CHAPTER 14

Take a bow

Step #8: Finale
The finale is everything a visitor leaves with, both tangible and intangible.

At the end of the movie *The Wizard of Oz*, Dorothy wakes up in her bed with Auntie Em and her beloved friends around her. It's a rewarding conclusion, as well as a surprise, to discover that everything in Oz was a dream. We see the Scarecrow, Tin Man, and Cowardly Lion in their regular farm clothes. But what if the movie had ended with Dorothy floating away from Oz in the balloon with the Wizard? We would have missed out on the sense of finale that all good stories have.

At the South Bark Dog Wash, the owners talk about their business as "the dog movie."[1] They have conceived of their experience as a film, with dog owners and their pets as the stars. Throughout the book *The Experience Economy*, Joseph Pine and James Gilmore compare running a business to putting together a theater production, using cast (workers), costumes (uniforms), and sets to create a memorable experience. If you think about your site as either a movie or a play, how should it end?

Screenwriting teacher Robert McKee suggests that great stories begin with a great ending. The writer then works backward to create all the plot points necessary to reach that ending in a fulfilling way.[2] In Chapter 5 we talked about creating your brand story. Look at that story now and decide what you think an appropriate ending would be. In the last scene of "the dog movie," customers go home with a clean and shiny pup and useful information on how to care for it. In Key West, Florida, visitors and locals make their way to Sunset Beach every night for the ritual of day's end. Think about a satisfying conclusion to *your* experience, and then make sure all the pieces further that story.

Closing the deal

The see-you-soon clause. In sales, the end of the deal is called "closing." A salesman might have given a customer every reason to want to buy a car but still has to ask, "What's it going to take to get you into this car today?" Museums and similar sites don't always remember to make a final pitch to visitors as they leave. Are you making it a point to verbally invite people to come back? If a family clearly had fun at your science center, that's a great time to ask if they'd like to buy a membership for next time or to tell them about upcoming events. Even if they say no, you've created the perfect opportunity to thank them for their visit, ask them how you could improve the experience, and tell them you're looking forward to seeing them again soon.

A beginning, a middle, and an end. Humans need rituals or ceremonies to mark arrivals and departures. In Japan, travelers used to receive gifts of travel money (called *senbetsu*) and in turn bring back gifts (*omiyage*). Western cultures mark comings and goings more casually. We say, "How was your trip?" "How was your weekend?" or "How was your day?"[3] One of the reasons the TV show *Survivor* has had such staying power is because it incorporates rituals. The host uses these exact words every episode as he extinguishes a player's torch: "The tribe has spoken. It's time for you to go." Creating your own ceremony—even a very simple one—for your visitors as they leave can have a powerful effect on the feeling they get as they complete their experience.

Thank them for bringing their family and friends, either with a small printed sign at the exit or with a slogan on a receipt. Or do it in person. Your appreciation actively encourages word-of-mouth advertising, which is the best kind you can receive. You can also reward visitors for referring interested people to your organization as members or donors. This is a great way to increase your visitor base just by doing what you do best. Make the process easy for visitors and the reward worth their effort. Give a departing visitor a coupon to pass on to a friend. It can be custom coded so that if the friend redeems the coupon, your loyal visitor gets the reward. This encourages people to pass coupons along to others they genuinely think would be interested, and it allows you to reward them when it happens.[4]

I once had a hairdresser who gave me $5 off for each of my friends who came to her for a haircut. If I referred five people to her, I got a free haircut. This was highly motivating to me, as well as nice thanks for the referrals. That same stylist also finished each cut by adding a complimentary sparkly bobby pin, which cost very little but added a wonderful finishing touch to the experience. Probably without realizing it, she gave me a souvenir of my salon experience—and a small ritual finale.

Souvenirs: A brief history of travel

Humans have taken trips to special places for thousands of years. While your site might not seem like a place worthy of a "pilgrimage," marketing expert Jon Schallert believes that even small businesses can recast themselves as destinations, drawing visitors from up to three hours away.[5] With this idea in mind, let's take a look at the role souvenirs have played in human history, so that you understand the importance of providing and creating the right "stuff" for people to take home.

Scenes from the pilgrimage trail. At first the motivation for people to travel was probably religious. They believed that visiting a holy place, like a shrine, would give them special protection, healing, or blessing. People came to believe that the holiness of a shrine could be transferred to them if they took home a piece of it. Rather than letting people break off stones or sacred bones, the guardians of those places started packaging tiny pieces of it—soil, water, holy oil, or fragments of bone—as relics. This helped protect the site and raise money to keep it maintained.[6]

By the Middle Ages, thousands of pilgrims were making the journey to the most famous shrine in Europe, the tomb of St. James at Santiago de Compostela in Spain. So many people made the trip—sometimes as many as half a million a year—that the "Way of St. James" became the first tourist route, complete with guidebooks, hostels, carved relics made of shiny black stone, and metal pilgrim badges. In what might be the first instance of corporate branding, the scallop shell became the "logo" for this pilgrimage, decorating pilgrims' hats, sculpture, architecture, and stained-glass windows along the roads to the tomb.[7]

Buying a memory. As an upper class emerged and began to travel in the 1600s, resorts like Spa in the Ardennes, Belgium, began selling luxury products to their wealthy guests: carved walking sticks, hairbrushes, inlaid boxes and tables, and mountain views engraved in glass. By the mid-1800s, more people were able to afford to travel, so seaside resort towns, where travelers would go to swim, rest, and shop began to spring up. Brighton Pier in England offered many of the same things you'd find on an oceanfront boardwalk now: sweets, telescopes, live music, and souvenirs like postcards and items to take home inscribed with "Brighton Pier." The first coin-pressing machines appeared in the late 1800s. These made it possible to create a unique souvenir by rolling a coin through plates that imprinted it with a design. The tradition continues today: pennycollector.com is a Web site that tells current collectors where they can find these machines in all fifty U.S. states and in more than thirty countries around the world.

As trains made travel affordable, amusement parks and international world's fairs became destinations for millions of people. Items made at the fairs showed off new technologies: visitors could watch their souvenirs being made on huge jacquard looms that wove bookmarks and in glass furnaces that produced paperweights. All kinds of other objects were branded with the fair's logo and colors.

Over the years, souvenirs became more strongly themed; characters, images, and logos were used to represent a brand: Mickey Mouse for Disney World, Elvis Presley at Graceland, Dolly Parton at Dollywood, even Monet's water lilies in museum shops. *Souvenir* is a French word meaning "to remember." So, while the word "souvenir" can mean cheap snow globes or plastic dinosaurs, in a crafted visitor experience the concept is a powerful one. It presents visitors with a tangible object to remember your site by.

Souvenir is a French word meaning "to remember." In a crafted visitor experience the concept is a powerful one. It presents visitors with a tangible object to remember your site by.

Create connections with souvenirs

Symbols of an experience. Souvenirs help people feel connected to meaningful times in their lives. You might think they aren't that important, but a study found that college students who decorated their dorm rooms with college memorabilia are more likely to graduate than those who decorated with things from home.[8] (And graduates are more likely to become donors, which is why colleges have spent millions in recent years to improve the dorm experience.)[9]

Hospitals sell logo-emblazoned sweatshirts and other memorabilia to patients and their families. Even funeral homes use pens with their names on them. These sites have found ways to turn their services, rather than the tragedies they often deal with, into brand-building opportunities.[10]

Showcase your icon. Is there an icon associated with your site—a famous view, a big dinosaur? If so, setting up a sign that says "Photo

Spot" is a great idea. The pictures people take there create permanent memories. It also means that people are getting an authentic experience, because that photo—with the visitor in it to prove she was there—could only have been taken in that spot. As images of your site proliferate, it adds to the value of both your experience and your visitors' photographs.[11] In many theme parks visitors are photographed at the climactic part of an adventure ride. As part of the Sydney Harbour Bridge Climb Experience in Australia, each guest is photographed at a high point in the climb with the Sydney Opera House in the background.[12]

The seafood restaurant chain Rockfish, in the southwest U.S., takes the photo-spot concept and flips it around brilliantly. Diners are encouraged to bring in photos of themselves fishing (usually while on vacation), which the restaurant frames and hangs on the walls. Patrons' happy vacation memories are then enshrined in the restaurant, creating a sense of "our place" or even "our booth." It's a powerful way to draw people to the restaurant again and again.[13] Are there ways you could incorporate your visitors' photos into your site, to create more of a sense of attachment?

People don't need souvenirs of experiences they can easily repeat, but they do want reminders of special experiences in order to bring the power and wonder of that experience home, just as the early pilgrims to Santiago de Compostela did. If you sell things that are available only at your site—not online or anywhere else—say so. It makes the souvenir exclusive and increases its value. Offer people objects that can become part of their collections (like enameled pins, spoons, or pencils). People then feel connected to your site, and you become a part of their collection at home, which is already important to them.[14]

Why people collect stuff

"I was there and I can prove it." Understanding why people create collections will help you decide what kinds of things to give away or sell. One motivation for collecting is "show and tell," the delight people take in proving they were actually *there*—at a famous or beautiful place. Sometimes people buy a souvenir because they are thinking about how it will look at home, and what stories they will be able to tell about it.[15] If your souvenir becomes part of someone's show and tell, then you have achieved word-of-mouth advertising through them.

My stuff therefore I am. People also collect things for status, to show that they're wealthy or have accomplished something in life. Material things help people define their self-worth; they're like mirrors that reflect who people are, what they like, and what their tastes are. Collectors are also part of a community. For men especially, collecting gives them the chance to compete with others by amassing the best "stuff."[16] Donors to arts organizations are rewarded with gold medals, lapel pins, and recognition in signage and on printed programs as symbols of both their status and their generosity.[17]

Collecting is aspiring. People also expand their sense of who they are—or who they can become—by the things they collect. One museum educator recalled being mesmerized by the National Gallery of Art in Washington, D.C., as a child. She bought postcards of all her favorite artworks and made her own "museum" in a book. She kept the book for twenty years, because it represented the moment she discovered what she wanted to be when she grew up.[18]

Collectors from birth. It's more common for kids to collect things than adults. Kids use souvenirs to discover and learn, prove their achievements (like finding unbroken sand dollars or arrowheads), play with or trade (pins, cards, or pencils), and wear (T-shirts and hats). When kids can find something to buy that can become part of their collections, it makes that purchase special.[19] Even children from highly religious homes can be collectors. In the ultra-orthodox Mea Shearim quarter of Jerusalem, kids are encouraged to collect and trade Torah Personalities cards with famous rabbis on them.[20]

Are you collectible? In our experience-driven culture, it's not surprising that people now collect experiences.[21] Some keep track of how many states, countries, or continents they have visited, or how many Hard Rock Cafe T-shirts they have. This trend is good for you, because it means that your experience, if it's memorable, might be one that people will want to collect for themselves.

Types of souvenirs

Researcher Beverly Gordon has identified five categories of souvenirs that people bring home.[22] I've numbered them, with number one being the things people are likely to keep longest, and number five being those that people will probably toss first.[23]

1. **Images.** Photos or postcards of a site visited are highly valued souvenirs. Photos tend to be kept for a long time, especially if the visitor is in the photo.

2. **Pieces-of-the-rock.** These are usually natural found objects: shells, beach glass, driftwood, or pinecones. But these objects can also be purchased; people buy fossils, pieces of old Comiskey Park in Chicago, sections of cable from the Brooklyn Bridge in New York, or bolts from the Statue of Liberty. Since they have the quality of authentic relics from a "holy" site, they too are often kept and treasured for a long time.

3. **Local products.** These are items unique to an area: food (Greek olives, Swiss chocolates), alcohol (Russian vodka or French wine), or crafts (huaraches from Mexico, enameled jewelry from Hong Kong). Handicrafts are kept as decorative items, but foods are usually eaten on special occasions. If the food is packaged in a special container, people might keep the container long after the food is gone.

4. **Markers.** Logo items like T-shirts, baseball caps, and sweatshirts with the name of a place on them are markers. They're usually given as gifts or used until they are worn out, then discarded.

5. **Symbolic shorthand.** These are items made expressly for sale, like miniature Eiffel Towers or salt and pepper shakers shaped like the Great Pyramids. These often fall into the junk or gag-gift category and aren't usually kept long, unless they are part of a collection.

Take-home materials

Anything visitors take with them when they leave your site is part of your brand, a key ingredient in your experience. For that reason, make sure that all your wrapping, bags, boxes, receipts, and handouts are of good quality and match the look of your other branded material. American museums were the first to create branded shopping bags, advertising both the museum and its current blockbuster exhibition. Luxury stores were quick to follow with branded bags of their own.[24]

Packaging the experience. In our culture we make gifts special by removing price tags and using special wrapping.[25] You can create a sense of specialness (researchers would call this a "sacred" or "holy" quality) by the way you wrap and present purchases to visitors. If you do this right, you can create that sense of "holiness transfer" I described at the beginning of the chapter. One woman reported that the "essence of Niketown follows you out the door." The gift she bought, wrapped in Niketown tissue and placed in a Niketown bag, made the T-shirt much more than just a T-shirt. So she was horrified when her brother, who was to deliver the gift for her, *unwrapped it in order to pack it*. She felt he'd "stripped [the intended receiver] of the Niketown-ness of the gift."[26] When you buy lingerie at Victoria's Secret, the bright pink bags, boxes, tissues, and black satin ribbon transfer the supermodel image of the brand to your home; buying similar lingerie at Wal-Mart doesn't feel the same. Consider what kind of aura you want to create and send home with your visitors.

Printing your message. You may be tempted to save money on printed materials by using cheap paper or "whipping something up" quickly. Don't do it. Remember that everything speaks. There are ways to keep printing costs down. First, make sure that you really need the flyer or brochure. Can you produce one high-quality printed piece instead of several cheaper ones? Can you make something small, or wallet-size instead of using a whole sheet of paper? Can items lead a double life as both useful take-home materials and souvenirs?

Avoid the problem of producing unbranded materials by having your graphic designer develop templates for handouts that you can produce on your computer. I've given details in Chapter 7. You can also print nicer brochures or maps and charge a small fee to cover the costs. And consider designing items that lend themselves to being cut up for scrapbooking, another popular trend. You might also provide templates on your Web site for this purpose. This increases the perceived value of ephemera and the likelihood that people will save them.[27] Use common sense and audience input when you're setting prices. And include your telephone number and Web address on everything you print.

Mementos

If you are successful at crafting a unique experience you'll make your visitor want to remember it in some physical way. While the terms "mementos" and "memorabilia" are generally thought of as being interchangeable, I use the terms in specific ways.

Mementos are free—or almost. When someone keeps an item like a postcard, theater program, or ticket stub, they have created a memento. Think of mementos as free pieces of the experience, ones that come with the rest of the package. We also use the terms "keepsake" or "token." These are items with little monetary value that are treasured because they bring back the memory of an experience. They tend to be more private items, perhaps stored in a box, photo album, or scrapbook. In San Diego, Loew's Coronado Resort gives away a photo album to teenage guests so that they can create their own branded memory books.[28] Found natural objects, like shells or rocks, are also mementos. (Mementos usually fall into the images or pieces-of-the-rock categories in Gordon's list.)

In recent years, devastating wildfires and hurricanes have destroyed thousands of homes in the U.S. When interviewed, people cried over the loss of their family photos, not their furniture or clothes. These mementos can't be bought; they're priceless. You might be able to go back and "do" the experience again but you can never recreate that unique moment in time.

Think about the pieces of your organization that could become mementos and make sure that they are of high quality and worth saving: ticket stubs, cash-register or other receipts, business cards, loyalty cards ("Buy 6, Get 1 Free"), special printed and dated programs, or posters.

Memorabilia

I consider memorabilia an additional item; something the visitor pays for—logo T-shirts, replicas, crafts, and pieces-of-the-rock, like fossils or bolts from the Statue of Liberty. Everything on Gordon's list can also qualify as memorabilia if it is for sale. (For example, souvenir photos or postcards are images, and packaged bolts are pieces-of-the-rock.) Again, the most important thing is to create high-quality merchandise that tells part of your story. Don't be afraid to charge more for this. It's better to have fewer high-quality items that represent your brand than a load of cheap junk. And it's good to sell at more than one price point, so that kids can always find something to buy. Just make sure that you are proud of everything you sell.

Starbucks has created some brilliant memorabilia by selling only high-end items (like their line of limited-edition teddy bears called

"Bearistas") and their Starbucks cards. The cards, which customers load with cash and use to speed up the checkout process, are also released in limited editions. New designs commemorate seasons, holidays, special events, or cross-promotions. People use the cards and then collect and trade them on eBay. Some limited-edition cards—with no monetary value—sell for over $100!

Let your store help support you. Sometimes nonprofit organizations think of selling memorabilia as a necessary evil, a way to pay for a "pure" mission. Many heritage sites have a row of independent hawkers selling cheap goods just outside their entrances, an approach that doesn't add anything positive to the experience. But without successful stores, the admission charge at many museums would have to skyrocket in order to keep the doors open. The Metropolitan Museum of Art grosses about $90 million a year from its stores and catalog sales. They estimate that without that revenue, admission would have to be about $75 per person.[29] If you're redesigning a nonprofit site, be sure that people can enter your store without paying admission. It will help you generate revenue by drawing shoppers who might not otherwise come to your site.

When you understand the important role that themed, high-quality memorabilia and mementos play in helping people feel connected to your site, you can choose items that support and enrich your visitors' experience and your bottom line. As you consider how you finish your experience—and extend it past people's stay time and into their homes and lives—remember that your goal is to become part of their lifestyle.

Conclusion

As I was writing this book, I continued to find examples of experience-based businesses popping up around the world. You can snow ski indoors in Dubai, sunbathe or camp in an indoor Tropical Islands theme park south of Berlin, or cruise on the Swedish Birka Line's *Paradise*, an enclosed tropical experience in the icy Baltic Sea.[30] You can fish in Florida with Captain Wes Rozier and the Fishin Chix, who sport hot-pink waders and fashionable clothes.[31] Or you can stop at the Cypress Creek Cafe in Wimberley, Texas, and be offered a glass of ice water to go when you leave. Ideas are all around you for ways to create memorable visitor experiences that are consistent with your organization's mission and theme.

Your experience-based organization. As you go about your workday, whether you exhibit art, teach hands-on science, run a state park, or manage a library, think about your visitors' needs and wants and how you can shape their visit with you as an experience. Consider your organizational theme and how you can weave it through every aspect of your visitors' time at your site. Use every opportunity to get feedback and input from your visitors. Find new partners who can help you increase your organization's reach through collaboration. Design your take-home message so that visitors know exactly who you are and what you stand for. And finally, have fun! Using Experience*ology* can re-energize you and your staff members to create a workplace that you enjoy every day, and that your visitors love returning to again and again.

How to use this book. Section 4, beginning on page 139, gives you detailed suggestions for using the exercises over the next weeks, months, or year and provides some helpful tools for organizing your work as you go. You'll find a summary of each chapter and exercises to help you apply the content to your site. I've also distilled supplementary readings for each chapter, recommending specific chapters from some of the best business books available if you want to delve deeper into a topic.

Tell me what you think

Please join the Experience*ology* community by visiting www.experienceology.com. You'll find more ideas in my blog, online classes, forums for discussing the book and sharing ideas with others, and helpful resources and links that extend the information from each chapter. Experience*ology* is a work in process, so please send me examples from your organization and your responses to the book. And thanks for reading!

How to use this book

If you've read the chapters, you already understand that a truly special visitor experience, one that is available nowhere else, is the way to meet your goals. Even if you already offer a great experience, you'll find ideas here for making it better. If your visitor experience is less than perfect, you know that you need to make changes, but you might not know where to begin. The exercises that follow will help you apply the information to your site. The outlines at the end of this section will lead you through the process of change. While each chapter builds on the previous ones, the chapters can stand alone. So, if one topic is particularly interesting to you, feel free to read that chapter or do those exercises first.

Starting the process

You can spend a few days or up to a full year working through the exercises. Decide how much time is realistic for you and your organization. Taking more time to work through the book will allow you to incorporate more changes and get deeper into the process. Doing it as a quick blitz can recharge your staff members and create new ways of thinking. The outlines that follow explain how to use the book over a year, six months, one month, or two days.

Creating your Experience*ology* binder

You're going to be generating lots of ideas and you'll need a place to collect them. Pick up a two-inch, three-ring binder to devote to the Experience*ology* process. Set up the following thirteen dividers:

- Mission and strengths
- Our experience
- Visitor behavior
- Creating our brand
- People first
- Invitation
- Welcome
- Orientation
- Comfort
- Communication
- Sensation
- Common sense
- Finale

When you discuss or work through each exercise, take notes, type them up, and then put them into the binder. You'll be reviewing your answers as you go along. By the time you finish the process you'll have an incredible resource for your organization.

Developing your Experience*ology* team

You can do the exercises with a group of staff members or by yourself. For some exercises, having a team of people for brainstorming will be more helpful than working alone. Those exercises are marked with the Brainstorming icon . If you are on your own and don't have a team, gather some people to help you brainstorm. When you are choosing people to help with the team-based exercises, look for those (family, friends, members) who want your organization to succeed.

Large organizations should have people from every level of the staff on the Experience*ology* team. Include at least one front-line staff person (from the sales, custodial, or maintenance teams). If you have more than fifteen staff members, you won't be able to include everyone at every meeting. Have people take turns so that everyone on your staff feels ownership of the process. It's important that the team isn't viewed as an elitist group. All your staff members create your visitor experience, so everyone has to buy into the process of change. If you have fewer than fifteen staff members, try to schedule meetings so that as many people as possible can take part.

If instructed, post things wherever the most people will see them. (Post copies in several locations if necessary.) A staff lounge is a great place to post information. Otherwise, an office is fine. Plan on taping items up on the wall when you need to brainstorm. You can do this in an office, conference room, team room, staff lounge, or even off-site.

Positive energy, humor, and lots of ideas. These are the essential ingredients needed for participating in the exercises. While you should try to include as many staff members as possible, people with negative attitudes will kill the process. If someone takes part in one meeting and brings the mood down, don't have that person participate again. (This may sound harsh, but you need positive attitudes for brainstorming and creating change. See Chapter 6 for more information on the importance of positive attitudes.)

If your business has stakeholders like a board of directors or cooperating association, you might want to include representatives from that group in some of the exercises marked with the Big Picture icon . These exercises focus on broad philosophical issues rather than operational ones. Report on your progress regularly to your stakeholders, as it shows that you're proactively managing your business to create greater visitor loyalty.

Using the exercises

Be prepared. It's helpful if everyone taking part in the exercises has read through the book before you begin holding meetings. That helps everyone understand how each chapter's exercises fit into the overall process. If it isn't possible for everyone to review the whole book, have people read the relevant chapter before working on a set of exercises.

If you're working as a group, one person should take the lead, organize the discussion, and keep the process on track. If possible, trade off facilitating with others who feel comfortable with that role, so that one person isn't viewed as "running" the process, but everyone sees it as theirs. To make the best use of people's time, distribute the questions before you meet so that people can think about their answers in advance. There are no right or wrong answers. Your organization is unique, and you are the experts.

Where to meet

You'll need a room that's big enough to hold your team, and space on the wall for posting sheets of paper. A dry-erase board or flipchart is helpful for some of the exercises. The calendar outlines (pages 143–53) list the supplies you'll need. You can meet over lunch if that works best. It helps to have snacks as a reward, or to plan a potluck meal. One organization that tested the exercises included wine and cheese in their Friday afternoon meetings. If possible, keep answers posted on the wall so that staff members can see the process evolve over time. In some cases you'll need to refer back to previous exercises, so having things posted in one place allows you to refer to them easily.

Money for changes

Since this is a new process, you won't have money set aside for making changes. As you do the exercises, it will become clear what kind of changes you need to make, what a practical timeline is, and how much making the changes will cost. Money might come from your budget for general operations or from funds earmarked for research and development, maintenance, marketing and public relations, new programs, or human-resources training. Jot down ideas for possible sources of funding as you go through the exercises.

Enlisting your experience testers

After you have completed Exercise 5C, review the description of your ideal visitors. Talk about where they live and how you might reach them. Ideally, you want to find three to ten potential visitors or family groups who represent your target visitors and ask them for feedback. Include families with small children (and have them bring their strollers) and people who use wheelchairs or walkers. If possible, include people with visual and hearing impairments.

Brainstorm ways you can reward them for helping you. Rewards can be free passes, discounts on merchandise, gift certificates, or actual merchandise. Base your reward on how much time and effort you ask of people. If you respect their time and boundaries, they'll love giving you their opinions.

Here are the things you want visitor feedback on:

- Directions to your site and your parking
- Your front entrance, greeting, and first impression
- How easily they can find their way around
- Body comfort issues: restrooms, food, and seating
- Mind comfort issues: How safe do they feel?
- How well you communicated with them
- How easily can they read and understand your signs?
- How well they feel your organization meets their needs
- Whether their "last impression" of your site is positive

One-year plan

	Month #1: Meeting date:	Month #2: Meeting date:	Month #3: Meeting date:
Preparation	Chapters 1–3	Chapter 4 Report on 3C	Chapter 5 Report on 4B–4E
Exercises to do	1A–1B, 2, 3A–3C	4A (if applicable), 4B–4E	5A–5D
Supplies needed	Flipchart Mission statement	Copy of *Changing for Good* (4A) Clipboard Flipchart	Posterboards Glue sticks Magazines
Assignments (if applicable)	3C:	4B: 4C: 4D:	5C: 5D:
Add to binder	Notes from 1A–1B, 2, 3A–3C	Notes from 4B–4E	Notes from 5A
Post	Mission, strengths and weaknesses	Four behavior-change objectives	Boards from 5B, 5C

One-year plan

	Month #4: Meeting date:	Month #5: Meeting date:	Month #6: Meeting date:
Preparation	Chapters 6 Review 5C, 5D (if applicable)	Chapter 7 Review 6C, 6D	Chapter 8 Review 7A, 7C
Exercises to do	6A–6D	7A–7C	8A–8C
Supplies needed	Flipchart or dry-erase board Organizational chart	Logo Every current print piece Screen shots from Web site Car	Clipboard Digital camera Digital image software
Assignments (if applicable)	6C: 6D:	7A: 7C:	8A: 8C:
Add to binder	Notes from 6A	Notes from 7A–7C	Notes from 8A–8C
Post	Organizational chart/Inverted pyramid Top five staff concerns	Logo redesign process (if applicable)	8A images and ideas

One-year plan

	Month #7: Meeting date:	Month #8: Meeting date:	Month #9: Meeting date:
Preparation	Chapter 9 Review 4B–4E, 8A, 8C	Chapter 10 Review 9A, 9C, 9D	Chapter 11 Review 10A–10C
Exercises to do	9A–9E	10A–10C	11A–11C
Supplies needed	Visitor map Clipboard Sticky notes Sticky arrows	Clipboard	Tape Flipchart or large dry-erase board Digital camera
Assignments (if applicable)	9A: 9C: 9D:	10A: 10B: 10C:	11B: 11C:
Add to binder	Notes from 9A–9E	Notes from 10A–10C	Notes from 11A–11C
Post			Theme sentence

One-year plan

	Month #10: Meeting date:	Month #11: Meeting date:	Month #12: Meeting date:
Preparation	Chapter 12 Review 6A, 11B, 11C	Chapter 13 Review 12B, 12C	Chapter 14 Review 13A–13D
Exercises to do	12A–12C	13A–13D	14A–14C
Supplies needed	Fun people Clipboard	Clipboard	Tape Flipchart or large dry-erase board Digital camera
Assignments (if applicable)	12B: 12C:	13A: 13B: 13C: 13D:	14A: 14B: 14C:
Add to binder	Notes from 12A–12C	Notes from 13A–13D	Notes from 14A–14C
Post		13C trends	

Six-month plan

	Month #1: Session #1:	Month #1: Session #2:	Month #2: Session #1:
Preparation	Chapters 1–2	Chapter 3 Review the progress on Exercise 2	Chapter 4
Exercises to do	1A, 1B, 2	3A–3C	4A (if applicable) 4B–4E
Supplies needed	Flipchart Mission statement	Flipchart	
Assignments (if applicable)		3C	4B: 4C: 4D: 4E:
Add to binder	Notes from 1A, 1B, 2	Notes from 3C	Notes from 4B–4E
Post	Mission, strengths and weaknesses		Four behavior-change objectives

Six-month plan

	Month #2: Session #2:	Month #3: Session #1:	Month #3: Session #2:
Preparation	Chapter 5	Chapter 6 Review 5C, 5D (if applicable)	Chapter 7 Review 6C, 6D
Exercises to do	5A–5D	6A–6D	7A–7C
Supplies needed	Posterboards Glue sticks Magazines	Flipchart or dry-erase board Organizational chart	Logo Every current print piece Screen shots from Web site Car
Assignments (if applicable)	5C: 5D:	6B: 6C: 6D:	7A: 7C:
Add to binder	Notes from 5A–5D	Notes from 6A	Notes from 7A–7C
Post	Boards from 5B, 5C	Organizational chart/Inverted pyramid Top five staff concerns	Logo redesign process (if applicable)

Six-month plan

	Month #4: Session #1:	Month #4: Session #2:	Month #5: Session #1:
Preparation	Chapter 8 Review 7A, 7C	Chapter 9 Review 4B–4E, 8A–8C	Chapter 10 Review 9A, 9C, 9D
Exercises to do	8A–8C	9A–9E	10A–10C
Supplies needed	Clipboard Digital camera Digital image software	Visitor map Clipboard Sticky notes Sticky arrows	Clipboard
Assignments (if applicable)	8A: 8B: 8C:	9A: 9C: 9D: 9E:	10A: 10B: 10C:
Add to binder	Notes from 8A–8C	Notes from 9A–9E	Notes from 10A–10C
Post	8A images and ideas		

Six-month plan

	Month #5: Session #2:	Month #6: Session #1:	Month #6: Session #2:
Preparation	Chapter 11 Review 10A–10C	Chapter 12 Review 11B, 11C	Chapters 13–14 Review 6A, 12B
Exercises to do	11A–11C	12A–12C	13A–13C, 14A–14C
Supplies needed	Tape Flipchart or large dry-erase board Digital camera	Fun people Clipboard	Clipboard Examples of all take-home items Flipchart or dry-erase board
Assignments (if applicable)	11B: 11C:	12B:	13B: 13C: 14C:
Add to binder	Notes from 11A–11C	Notes from 12A–12C	Notes from 13A–13C, 14A–14C
Post	Theme sentence		

One-month or Quarterly plan

	Meeting #1:	Meeting #2:	Meeting #3:
Preparation	Chapters 1–4	Chapters 5–6 Review 4B, 4D	Chapters 7–10 Review 5C (if applicable), 6D
Exercises to do	1A, 1B, 2, 3A, 4B, 4D	5C, 5D, 6A, 6D	7B, 7C, 8A, 9A, 9E, 10A–10C
Supplies needed	Flipchart Mission statement	Posterboards, glue sticks Magazines Flipchart or dry-erase board Organizational chart	Every current print piece Screen shots from Web site Car, clipboard, digital camera Digital image software
Assignments (if applicable)	4B: 4D:	5C: 6D:	10A: 10B: 10C:
Add to binder	Notes from 1A, 1B, 2, 4B, 4D	Notes from 5B, 5C, 6A, 6D	Notes from 7B, 7C, 8A, 9A, 9E, 10A–10C
Post	Two behavior-change objectives	Top five staff concerns Boards from 5B, 5C	8A images and ideas

One-month or Quarterly plan

	Meeting #4:	Follow-up in one month:	Follow-up in six months:
Preparation	Chapters 11–14 Review 7C, 8A, 9E, 10A–10C	Review 11B, 12B, 14A	Review 4B, 4D, 6D, 7C, 10C, 14B, 14C
Exercises to do	11B, 12A, 12B, 13A, 14A	14B, 14C	7B, 7C, 8A, 9A, 9E, 10A–10C
Supplies needed	Digital camera Clipboard Flipchart Tape	Examples of all take-home items Flipchart or dry-erase board	
Assignments (if applicable)	11B: 12B: 14A:		
Add to binder	Notes from 11B, 12A, 12B, 13A, 14A		
Post	13A lists		

Two-day blitz or Full-day retreat

	Day #1:	Day #2: Or Full-day retreat:	Follow-up in one month:
Preparation	Read all chapters Organize food and supplies	Organize food and supplies	Review 4B, 4D Review items assigned from Day #2
Exercises to do	1A, 1B, 2, 3A, 4B, 4D, 5B, 6A	7C, 8A, 9A, 9E, 10A, 10B, 11B, 12B, 14A, 14B	If possible: 5C, 6B–6D, 11A, 12A, 13C
Supplies needed	Flipchart Mission statement Posterboards, glue sticks Magazines	Car Clipboard Digital camera Examples of all take-home items	
Assignments (if applicable)	4B: 4D:	Assign one person to follow up on any items identified during the exercises	
Post	Two behavior-change objectives Board from 5B Top five staff concerns		
Notes:			

Chapter 1 Summary

- Our economy has changed. Your visitors' expectations have changed. If you serve the public, you are now also in the business of selling experiences.

- The better your visitors' experiences, the more successful your site will be.

- A poor experience will impact you as lost business. An unhappy visitor tells an average of ten other people about a problem with you. You can't afford that kind of bad publicity.

- The average company loses twenty percent of its customers every year.

- Analyzing your site from the visitor's point of view helps you to keep visitors, increase revenue, and stay competitive.

Further Reading for Chapter 1

- *Legacy* magazine, published by the National Association of Interpretation. The interpretive experience issue, vol. 16, no. 6 (November-December 2005). Articles apply the content of *The Experience Economy* (see below) to interpretive sites like parks.

- B. Joseph Pine II and James H. Gilmore, *The Experience Economy: Work Is Theatre & Every Business a Stage*.

  Chapter 1—"Welcome to the Experience Economy"—defines the trend toward experience-based businesses.

- *Public Garden* magazine, published by the American Public Garden Association. The changing visitor experience issue, no. 2 (November 21, 2006). Articles review experiences in public gardens.

- Bernd H. Schmitt, *Customer Experience Management: A Revolutionary Approach to Connecting with Your Customers*.

  Chapter 8—"Delivering a Seamlessly Integrated Customer Experience"— provides advice for analyzing your own experience; illustrates how the details add up.

- Visit www.experienceology.com for additional links, and listings of books, articles, and classes about experience-based businesses.

Exercise 1A:

Why should they pick you?

- Name all the reasons your site is great.

- List all your leisure-time competition within one hour's drive.

- Describe all the ways you are unique and offer a better experience than your competitors. Mark your greatest strengths on the list with stars.

Exercise 1B:

Rating your strengths and weaknesses

- List all the weaknesses you see in your site in any order they come to mind. Put a star by the weaknesses you think are most significant.

- You now have two lists: strengths (from 1A) and weaknesses (from 1B), sorted by stars into high and low priority. When you type up your notes from this meeting, put all the starred weaknesses together at the top of your "Weaknesses" list. Put all the starred strengths at the top of your "Strengths" list.

- Over the next few months, focus on improving your primary weaknesses, while using your best strengths. Post your lists in your team room or office and refer to them regularly as you work through this book.

Chapter 2 Summary

- The visitor experience takes place in two dimensions. First it happens inside your visitors. It's occurring from their point of view, created by a combination of feelings, sensations, and prior experiences. Second, many separate pieces outside a visitor make up the visitor experience.

- Integrating those pieces is key to creating a great experience.

- The experience is only as good as the weakest piece, so all the details matter.

- The process of creating a great experience can be broken down into eight steps, which follow a visitor's visit from start to finish.

- Having a mission statement clarifies your specific audience, your purpose as a business, and the area you serve, all of which combine to create a unique, integrated experience.

Further reading for Chapter 2

- Jim Collins and Jerry I. Porras, *Built to Last: Successful Habits of Visionary Companies.*

  Chapter 11—"Building the Vision"— gives examples of vision statements of famous companies and gives advice on how to craft your own statement.

- Mary Kay Cunningham, *The Interpreters Training Manual for Museums.*

  Chapter 1—"Lay the Foundation"— addresses mission statements as an important foundation for interpretation.

- Disney Institute, *Be Our Guest: Perfecting the Art of Customer Service.*

  Chapter 1—"Service, Disney Style"— presents a succinct overview of how Disney creates seamless experiences through fanatical attention to detail.

- John H. Falk and Lynn D. Dierking, *The Museum Experience.*

  Section 4—"A Professional's Guide to the Museum Experience"—is an overview of the entire museum experience from museum-learning gurus.

- Paco Underhill, *Why We Buy: The Science of Shopping.*

  Chapter 18—"The Self-Exam"—shows you how to review your own experience from a "retail anthropology" perspective.

- Visit www.experienceology.com for additional links and listings of books, articles, and classes about the visitor experience.

Exercise 2:

Defining your mission

- If you already have a mission statement, review it now. If you do not have one, write no more than three sentences about what your site's overall goal is. This mission statement should answer the question "Why are we here?" This drafted statement will get more focused as you work through the exercises in this book. Your mission statement should include:

  - your target audience (or audiences)
  - your purpose
  - the geographic area you serve

- The process of creating a mission statement can get sticky when people focus on reworking the text over and over, missing the big picture. Don't fuss over the language; just get something in writing. Think of it as a living document, rather than something that will be carved in stone. In *Built to Last*, authors Jim Collins and Jerry Porras offer this suggestion for getting to the deeper meaning of your mission. Once you have drafted a rough mission statement, ask, "Why is that important?" After you answer the question, ask it four more times. (This can be done over several meetings and will help you distill your mission to its essence.)

- Post a draft of your mission statement, and each revision, so that everyone on your staff can refer to the evolving document regularly.

Chapter 3 Summary

- Free time is a precious and limited commodity. Americans devote roughly five hours a day to leisure activities. About three of those five hours are spent watching TV.

- People are looking for at least one of these leisure-time rewards from your business:

  1) social interaction

  2) active participation

  3) comfortable surroundings

  4) challenging, new, or unusual experiences

  5) opportunities to learn

  6) doing something worthwhile

- According to authors Joseph Pine and James Gilmore, the experience a business offers can be educational, entertaining, esthetic, or escapist.

- Your visitors are looking for **authentic experiences** and **personal rewards** when they interact with you.

- If you can, enlarge the scope of your site and become a "third place." By doing so you can cater to anyone who lives within walking distance, even if you haven't thought of them as visitors before.

Further reading for Chapter 3

- Gail Anderson, ed., *Reinventing the Museum: Historical and Contemporary Perspectives on the Paradigm Shift*.

  Essay 12—"Staying Away: Why People Choose Not to Visit Museums" by Marilyn Hood—is a classic study identifying key differences between people who visit museums and those who don't.

  Essay 13—"A Visitor's Bill of Rights" by Judy Rand—defines key aspects of every museum visit.

- Seth Godin, *All Marketers Are Liars: The Power of Telling Authentic Stories in a Low-Trust World*.

  Step 4—"Great Marketers Tell Stories We Believe"

  Step 5—"Marketers with Authenticity Thrive"

  Both sections reveal more on the relationship among authenticity, storytelling, and marketing.

- B. Joseph Pine II and James H. Gilmore, *The Experience Economy: Work Is Theatre & Every Business a Stage*.

  Chapter 2—"Setting the Stage"— describes the four realms of experiences and is rich with examples.

- You'll find additional links and listings of books, articles, and classes that relate to this chapter at www.experienceology.com.

Exercise 3A:
What do you have to offer?

- Describe how you offer your visitors each of the six rewards below. Write "none" if something doesn't apply.

  1. We encourage social interaction.

  2. Our visitors can participate in an active way.

  3. We help visitors feel comfortable in our surroundings.

  4. Our visitors enjoy the challenge of a new or unusual experience.

  5. We provide learning opportunities.

  6. When visitors spend time with us, they are doing something worthwhile.

- After listing your answers, brainstorm ways to improve or expand your performance in each area. Some of these payoffs might not apply to your site, but you might come up with something creative that adds depth to your experience.

Exercise 3B:
Describe your experience

- Offering a well-rounded experience (Exercise 3A) will help you compete with other leisure-time businesses in your area. Circle the description(s) that best describes your site:

- **Educational:** We teach our visitors new things.

- **Entertainment:** Our visitors sit back and watch our experience.

- **Esthetic:** Our visitors absorb the beauty of our experience.

- **Escapist:** Our visitors create their own unique experience each time.

- Now make a list of other local businesses in each category you circled. Send a team member to investigate each one and report back to the group. What are those businesses doing better than you are? Where do you excel? What ideas can you borrow? This will help you focus on offering a unique experience that will draw your visitors off their couches and into your site.

Exercise 3C:
Capitalize on the seasons

- Consider longer daylight hours (and off-season television programming) as an opportunity. Is your site open when people are available and looking for something new? Why not shift your hours and try to capture some of your potential visitors' free time?

- If you have an indoor site, you might draw more people when it rains, so plan special programs to capitalize on busy rainy days. Outdoor sites will be busier in nice weather.

- During holiday seasons, how can you add special services that provide value to your busy visitors? Can you add gift-wrapping, shipping, or another service that meets multiple needs? How can you draw people to you instead of to the mall? Consider working with a for-profit company to add some services for the holiday season.

Chapter 4 Summary

- The first key to getting visitors to come back is to recognize that you are trying to influence their behavior. Being clear about what kinds of behavior you are trying to influence is the first step toward achieving your goal.

- In the **self-help** area of behavior change, people go through six stages to successfully change a behavior. If it fits your site, you can help them decide that they have a problem, provide support and information as they prepare to change, focus on their success, or help them maintain their changed lifestyle.

- You can use **persuasion** tactics to help influence the way visitors respond to your offerings.

- **Frequency** is how often a visitor comes to your site.

- **Duration** describes the length of time you want visitors to spend with you.

- **Engagement** is what you want them to do while they are at your site.

- **Off-site actions** are things you want them to do after they leave.

Further reading for Chapter 4

- Peter C. Honebein and Roy F. Cammarano, *Creating Do-It-Yourself Customers: How Great Customer Experiences Build Great Companies*.

  Chapter 3—"The Roots of Coproduction Experience Design"—lists six "weapons of influence" key to behavior change.

- Don Peppers and Martha Rogers, *Enterprise One to One: Tools for Competing in the Interactive Age*.

  Chapter 2—"Some Customers Are More Equal Than Others"—is a valuable guide to determining the lifetime value of a customer; helps you stratify customers according to spending habits; is useful for development.

- James O. Prochaska, John C. Norcross, and Carlo C. DiClemente, *Changing for Good: A Revolutionary Six-Stage Program for Overcoming Bad Habits and Moving Your Life Positively Forward*.

  This is an excellent resource for sites engaged in conservation psychology; it helps you understand how to move people toward change.

- Shaun Smith and Joe Wheeler, *Managing the Customer Experience: Turning Customers into Advocates*.

  Chapter 2—"Beyond Satisfaction"—gives strategies for increasing brand loyalty.

- Paco Underhill, *Why We Buy: The Science of Shopping*.

  Chapter 16—"Magic Acts"—shows you how to create displays that influence shopping behavior.

Exercise 4A:
Using self-help to your advantage

- If you read the description about the six stages of behavior change and said, "Yes! I can use this!" then you should get a copy of *Changing for Good*. To get started now, reread my summary of the six stages beginning on page 34. Picture your visitors going through those stages. How can you provide additional products, services, support, or programs that meet their needs?

- A garden, zoo, or park could develop specific programs targeted at increasing earth-friendly lifestyles for each of the five stages, estimating which visitor groups are likely to be in each stage. Convention-tour audiences are most likely to be in the pre-contemplation stage, lecture-tour audiences in the contemplation stage, and travelers on ecotours in the action stage.

Exercise 4B:
How often do they visit?

- Complete this statement: "In a perfect world, our visitors would visit us _____ times per _____." This is your **ideal frequency**.

- Pick ten or twenty visitors at random for a week, asking each one when they last visited. **Actual frequency** is: _____ times per _____.

- Compare your ideal to your actual frequency. How close are you to your ideal?

- Now develop a plan to improve your actual frequency and move it closer to your ideal. Try loyalty cards, weekly or monthly specials, "Ten-Percent Off" coupons on the next visit

(or the next purchase in your store), or free admission for a friend when your visitor returns. Include an action plan with an internal timeline for implementing it.

Exercise 4C:
How long do they stay?

- Complete this statement: "In a perfect world, our visitors would spend _____ hours and _____ minutes visiting us." This is your **ideal duration**.

- You probably don't know the actual average duration of your visitors' stays, unless your museum has done extensive tracking and timing studies (and those are usually done just for a single exhibition). Keep a log of people's visits over the next few days or week, noting how long visitors stay. If you have a retail operation, note how many people leave without buying. Most stores don't know their conversion rate (the percentage of browsers who turn into buyers) but it's a key component of a successful retail business. **Actual duration**: _____ hours and _____ minutes.

- Compare your ideal to your actual duration. Set an objective to get you closer to your ideal. Include an action plan with a timeline for implementing it.

Exercise 4D:
How engaged are they?

- Make a list of visitor behaviors that you would like to see at your site. This includes actions like getting questions answered by a staff member, reading wall labels or interpretive texts, and socializing with others in their group—laughing, sitting, playing, or reading out loud.
- Set a specific objective that you can measure to encourage one or more of these behaviors. Include an action plan with a timeline for implementing it.

Exercise 4E:
What do they do when they leave?

- Make a list of any behavior you would like to encourage in your visitors **when they are off-site**. These behaviors might include telling friends about you, making plans to come back, deciding to renew their membership, or taking part in some kind of activity that aligns with your mission.
- Set a specific, measurable objective to encourage one or more of these behaviors. Include an action plan with a timeline for implementing it.
- Take a look at each of the four behavior-change objectives you have set using Exercises 4B–4E. Brainstorm how each can be implemented. Which departments will take part in the effort? What kind of support will they need?

Post these on the wall:

Our frequency objective is:

Our duration objective is:

Our engagement objective is:

Our off-site behavior objective is:

Chapter 5 Summary

- Every aspect of your business, from your name to your building and everything in it, creates your "brand." The sum total of the impressions you make on a visitor defines your brand in the visitor's mind. A brand is not simply a logo or a slogan.

- Branding is a process of **creating a story** about your operation to set it apart from your competition.

- At the core of your brand story is the **promise** you make to your visitors.

- Negative aspects of branding in the corporate world include disrespect for customers and employees, overpriced goods, and no spaces left free of logos.

- Positive aspects of branding include using the power of stories to draw visitors to you, creating connections and dialogue with your visitors, and applying the power of a brand for the greater good of society.

- For cultural institutions, branding is an essential tool for competing with other leisure destinations.

- As part of a branding exercise, consider whether your organization's name truly captures your personality and meets your goals, mission, and vision.

Further reading for Chapter 5

- David F. D'Alessandro, *Brand Warfare: 10 Rules for Building the Killer Brand.*

  Rule 1: "It's the Brand, Stupid"—is a primer on branding with hilarious cautionary tales.

- Marc Gobé, *Emotional Branding.*

  Chapter 11—"Emotionally Charged Identities—Unforgettable Brand Personalities"

  Chapter 17—"d/g*'s Recipes for Emotional Branding Strategies"

  This excellent study shows you how to convey your site's "personality" through a dynamic logo; create "aspirational customer" boards; and learn from famous companies that have successfully rebranded themselves.

- Duane Knapp and Gary Sherwin, *Destination BrandScience* (available only through www.iacvb.org).

  Chapter 1—"What a Brand Is—And Is Not"

  Chapter 3—"Objective Brand Assessment for Destinations"

  Reference section—"The BrandScience™ Guide for Destination RFPs"

  This is a back-to-basics instruction booklet for strengthening your brand.

- James B. Twitchell, *Branded Nation.*

  Chapter 4—"Museumworld: The Art of Branding Art"—discusses branding in museums: the good, the bad, and the ugly.

Exercise 5A:
What's in a name?

- Ask three people who have never been to your site to give you their impressions simply from hearing your organization's name. If they have heard of you but have never visited, ask them for details about what they would expect to see and do if they did come. Negative impressions can offer the most useful information. You can often overcome people's hesitations about sharing negative feedback by assuring them they won't hurt your feelings and that you want their honest opinion. It helps to say, "We've received complaints about X. What do you think?"

- Discuss the reactions you got with your team. How did the responses measure up against your mission?

Exercise 5B:
Defining your brand

- If your **organization** were a person, describe that person's personality: Are they male or female? What kind of car would they drive? What kind of music would they listen to? What kind of pets would they have? How would their house be decorated?

- Get a large posterboard and fill it with images and words (from magazines, catalogs, or the Internet) that help convey your organizational personality. Have everyone on your staff contribute images and words.

- Post the board in your office or team room.

Exercise 5C:
Your target visitors

- Think about who your **visitors** are. Do they fit into one group, like "families within walking distance?" Or two major groups, like "families from the Bay Area" and "Latinos from the Bay Area?" Develop a visitor profile board, like the one you developed for your organization in Exercise 5B, for each target group.

- Use these boards to help you stay focused on your target audience(s) whenever you are planning programs or printing materials; changing your interior design; making new signs; ordering merchandise for your store; or developing marketing or public-relations materials. You'll use these boards in several of the exercises for Chapters 7–14.

- Post the board(s) in your office or team room.

- If you are a large site with a complex visitor base, you may need to hire a firm that specializes in market segmentation to help you define your audience in a thorough and sophisticated way. Visit www.experienceology.com for recommendations.

Exercise 5D: !

Do you need help?

- As you discuss your organization's personality, how appealing is it to you? To your target visitors? Does your name convey your personality exactly? If the answer to these questions is no, consider changing your name.

- If you feel your name or personality is not appealing to your visitors, your brand identity might need some expert help. The reading list will help you get started. If you can't afford a branding consultant, see if you can get the services donated, or trade a branding consultation for something your business can provide. If you do have to spend money, it doesn't have to be a fortune; even small changes, if they're well implemented, can make a difference.

Chapter 6 Summary

- Passion and positive attitudes are free.

- All visitors should be greeted warmly, with a smile, as if each is a welcome guest.

- Hire people with great attitudes and smiles who are passionate about life. They can always be trained for other skills. Pessimistic, cynical people can't give great customer service. Period.

- Include time in your staff-training process, especially time spent with the top people in your organization. Employees know they are valued if you spend time with them.

- Trust your employees; share information and don't constrain them with rules. If you've done a good job of hiring and training, they will not let you down.

- Show your employees they are valued with creative perks and rewards. Allow them to create office spaces they feel comfortable in and encourage healthy behaviors during and after work.

Further reading for Chapter 6

- Chip Bell and Bilijack Bell, *Magnetic Service: Secrets for Creating Passionately Devoted Customers.*

  Secret #5—"Give Customers an Occasional Miracle"—details rich examples of stellar, personalized customer service that are both memorable and repeatable.

- Jim Collins and Jerry I. Porras, *Built to Last: Successful Habits of Visionary Companies.*

  Chapter 6—"Cult-Like Cultures"—examines great companies that have strong internal cultures employees either love or leave.

- Disney Institute, *Be Our Guest: Perfecting the Art of Customer Service.*

  Chapter 3—"The Magic of the Cast"— tells how to cast the right people for front-line jobs; gives detailed customer-service guidelines.

- Kevin Freiberg and Jackie Freiberg, *Guts! Companies That Blow the Doors Off Business-as-Usual.*

  Chapter 3—"Gutsy Leaders Create a Sense of Ownership"

  Chapter 4—"Gutsy Leaders Hire People Who Don't Suck"

  Learn how to improve your staffing practices from top maverick companies.

- Visit www.experienceology.com for additional links and listings of books, articles, and classes to help you empower your staff.

Exercise 6A:
A "people first" assessment

- *Note: Do this exercise **only** if upper management is fully committed to change. If necessary, the exercise can be done anonymously. If staff members feel comfortable sharing negative feedback only in private, you'll know that morale is low, so it's even more important to do this exercise. Proceed carefully, making sure that you create a process that safeguards staff members' anonymity. Otherwise the staff will have another reason to feel that their opinions aren't valued, damaging morale even further.*

- Make a list of the top staff concerns. Post them in your team room or office and invite everyone to add their comments. At the end of a week, review all the comments and reorder the list, with the most pressing staff concern in the #1 spot. Choose the top five concerns to work on over the next six months. Review this exercise in six months and see if you have made progress.

- Rate your organization on how well your staff members are treated. Consider these questions: How is morale? How rested and energetic is your staff? Are people taking vacations? Are people pursuing education and training? How engaged do staff members become in meetings? Do they offer suggestions for improvements? Have each staff member submit their comments, and share all the responses among staff. You can have people type up comments and put them into a box if they don't feel comfortable being identified.

Exercise 6B:
Turn your organizational chart on its head

- If you have an organizational chart, post a copy of it on the wall of your office or team room. Now create your own "inverted pyramid" next to it, with your *visitors at the top*. Front-line staff will be the next most important level. The bottom of the pyramid is the executive director or board of directors. If you have more than four or five levels, your business is management heavy and may be out of touch with both visitors and front-line staff.

- The task at each level is to support the work of the level above it. If you are committed to organizational change, this can be a powerful tool to improving the experience you offer.

- Take a look at staff functions as they now appear on your inverted pyramid. Can people be cross-trained to provide a better visitor experience? Are your job and departmental categories meaningful to your visitor? How can you make the most of the people you have on your staff?

Exercise 6C:
Tweak your training

- Have staff members on each level of the inverted pyramid work on their own training plan. Keep in mind that the goal is to fully support and empower the people at the next level up. Executives/directors/ department heads will train each other to support their managers. The managers will train each other to support the front-line staff. The front-line staff will train each other to support the customers.

Exercise 6D:
Perks and rewards

- Create six small teams or temporary committees, ideally from people who volunteer for the task. Give each team a one-month deadline to report on their progress. Make sure they have the list of the top five staff concerns (from Exercise 6A) to incorporate into their work. Each team works on one of the following:

  1. Improving office space and working conditions
  2. Decorating the office
  3. Assuring employee health, fitness, and safety
  4. Establishing a time-off policy
  5. Planning for celebrations
  6. Exploring training and educational opportunities

Chapter 7 Summary

- Just as a party invitation gives a wealth of detail about an upcoming experience, your organization's invitation helps visitors understand what you have to offer.

- The better you understand your target visitors, the more appropriate your invitation will be.

- The foundation of your organizational identity is your logo. You should have only one.

- Every print piece you produce and Web page you host should be part of a coordinated invitation. While they don't need to match exactly, a consistent identity should link them all.

- Hire the best graphic designer you can afford to develop your identity and logo. At the end of the project the designer should leave you with an identity-standards manual that provides you with clear guidelines for maintaining a consistent identity. You will want to put the identity standards into play as soon as you receive them and pass them on to designers who may work for you in the future.

- If possible, coordinate your directional street signs and parking lot with your identity standards.

Further reading for Chapter 7

- Sean Adams and Noreen Morioka, *Logo Design Workbook: A Hands-On Guide to Creating Logos.*

  Chapter 6—"Logo Development"

  Chapter 7—"System Dynamics"

  This manual assists you with getting started on a new logo, with or without a graphic designer.

- Duane Knapp and Gary Sherwin, *Destination BrandScience* (available only through www.iacvb.org).

  Chapter 1—"What a Brand Is—And Is Not"

  Chapter 3—"Objective Brand Assessment for Destinations"

  Reference section—"The BrandScience™ Guide for Destination RFPs"

  This is a back-to-basics instruction booklet for strengthening your brand. The assessment guidelines will help you make your invitation more focused and powerful.

- Robin Williams, *The Non-Designer's Design Book.*

  This gives you a practical way to greatly improve the look of all your print materials.

- My Web site, www.experienceology. com, offers additional links and listings of books, articles, and classes on the invitation.

Exercise 7A:

Designing your invitation

- Take a look at your organization's logo. If you have more than one, put them all up on the wall to examine. Compare your existing logo(s) with your name and personality. Consider how your ideal visitors might respond to your logo. If you feel your logo isn't doing the job—or you decided on a name change while working on Chapter 5—work with a graphic designer to develop a new logo.

Exercise 7B:

Analyze what you've got

- Collect one copy of every single print piece you currently hand out. Print off some pages in color from every section of your Web site as well. Put all these up on the wall alongside your visitor and personality boards and your logo(s). Measure them against what your organization is trying to achieve. Any one of them might be a great piece and be quite well designed. But if they don't suit your new identity, plan to have them redesigned as soon as your budget permits.

Exercise 7C:

Take a drive

- Get in a car and drive about a mile away from your site. Now approach your site as if you were going there for the first time. How easily can you find it? Can you easily see where to park? Are your signs doing a great job of inviting people in? Are people on foot getting a clear invitation too?

- If you have a destination business, like a tourist attraction, museum, garden, park, or zoo, you will want to start farther away. Drive five or ten miles away from your site and check the signage as you come back in. Have one member of your team drive in from the nearest highway and report back to you. On another day, try using an unusual route for this exercise, to give you a fresher perspective.

- Park in your visitor lot if you have one. Was it clear from the street where to turn? Could you easily tell where the front entrance was when you got out of the car? Before coming inside, brainstorm ways to make your parking area fit better with your organization's theme.

- If you don't have your own parking lot, be sure to include detailed parking suggestions on your Web site, print pieces, and voice-mail system.

- Discuss whether or not the street-signage component of your invitation needs to be improved. This is a long-term project, as street signage often requires approval from city, county, provincial, or state authorities. Assign a priority to this project (high, medium, or low), and make one person responsible for it. Have them report their progress monthly.

Chapter 8 Summary

- Your front door should be clearly visible from half a block away and convey to visitors who you are and what you have to offer them.

- If you don't have one, consider creating an advance organizer—visual shorthand for what your site is about—to tell visitors what you have to offer.

- Your front door should be easy to open. Keep the information you post at the doorway—like your name and operating hours—brief.

- The first person a visitor sees should be friendly and welcoming.

- All visitors should be greeted like guests, with a warm smile.

- Follow the guidelines in Chapter 6 to hire great people, especially those who are part of your visitors' first impression.

- Include all front-line staff (security people, volunteers, custodians, customer-service representatives, and food-service workers) in staff training and parties; continue to give them information about your brand and your mission as it evolves.

Further reading for Chapter 8

- Mary Kay Cunningham, *The Interpreters Training Manual for Museums.*

  Chapter 3—"The Ultimate Interpreter: Creating Expectations and Standards"

  Module 1—"An Interpretive Overview" (suitable for all front-line staff members)

  This valuable resource presents a self-contained training curriculum for all your front-line staff.

- Malcolm Gladwell, *Blink: The Power of Thinking Without Thinking.*

  Introduction—"The Statue That Didn't Look Right"—explores perceptions and first impressions; the Getty's forged statue is discussed as a case study in trusting your instincts.

- Betsy Sanders, *Fabled Service: Ordinary Acts, Extraordinary Outcomes.*

  This is a must-read on customer service and greetings from Nordstrom's top trainer.

- Additional links, and listings of books, articles, and classes on the welcome are available on www.experienceology.com.

Exercise 8A:
Attention grabbers

- Go outside and walk half a block away from your front entrance. Imagine that you're trying to find your site for the first time. Does the entrance clearly get your attention? Can you tell what kind of facility it is? How would your entrance draw in a new (targeted) visitor? How well does it convey your personality? Does the entrance feel intimidating or welcoming?

- Brainstorm different ways to add to your entrance or building to get the attention of passersby. Can you create an oversize icon, large banner, or other advance organizer?

- Consider adding trees to your streetscape, and have existing trees pruned properly so they don't obscure your welcome.

- Use a computer program like PowerPoint, Illustrator, or Photoshop to play around with ideas by cutting and pasting mockups of icons or signs over a photo of your entrance. This allows you to try out new ideas for free until you have something that excites you.

- Are your window displays effective for drivers as well as for people on foot?

Exercise 8B:
Your front door

- From outside, head to your front door and check the signage. Remember that visitors will be moving as they read your signs. Are you trying to communicate too much? Should the typeface be larger or a different color?

- Is the door easy to open? Even for people pushing a stroller or using a wheelchair?

Exercise 8C:
Analyze your first impression

- Step inside your front door or entrance. What is the first thing you see? Is it fresh, inviting, and well organized? Do you need to spruce things up?

- *(Do this next step privately, not by standing in front of your greeter.)* Put yourself in your visitor's place and evaluate the first person she sees. Is the greeter friendly and warm? If it's a security guard, is this the best first impression?

- If the current situation is not ideal, decide whether customer-service training and coaching would help. This is a delicate topic and needs to be handled sensitively. Give people on your staff a chance to become more aware of the visitors' perspective before you decide to reassign them. You will probably find that people often evaluate themselves more harshly than others might and are eager to improve. Having all front-line staff members take part in these exercises can also help everyone understand that changes are necessary for the success of the site and aren't to be taken personally.

Chapter 9 Summary

- The **transition zone** is the first area visitors hit when they enter your site—when they are still adjusting to the new atmosphere. Shorten the zone using sound, lighting, and visual cues. Don't waste signs, greeters, or flyers until visitors are past the zone.

- People tend to **turn right and reach right**. Keep the right-hand bias in mind when you design the layout of your site.

- Maps should include icons and landmarks used on site. "You Are Here" maps should always be designed so they match the direction the viewer is facing.

- Good wayfinding signs use icons, color-coding, and simplified names. Divide your site into five to seven regions for the most effective wayfinding system.

- Test placement of signs when visitors are present. Consider including signs on lesser-used routes and in both directions of travel.

- Eliminate the "butt-brush effect" so visitors feel comfortable when they're looking at displays.

- Avoid creating a "shallow loop"; place something popular in the back of your site.

Further reading for Chapter 9

- Disney Institute, *Be Our Guest: Perfecting the Art of Customer Service*.

  Chapter 4—"The Magic of Setting"— contains expert tips from the inventors of the theme park on how to move people smoothly along.

- Wayne Hunt, *Environmental Graphics: Projects & Process*.

  This excellent book gives endless illustrated examples to help you solve wayfinding challenges. It's out of print, but you can locate it through libraries and some online vendors.

- Rachel Kaplan, Stephen Kaplan, and Robert L. Ryan, *With People in Mind: Design and Management of Everyday Nature*.

  Chapter 4—"Wayfinding"—contains practical ideas for moving people comfortably through outdoor sites.

- For additional orientation resources, visit www.experienceology.com.

Exercise 9A:
Identify your transition zone

- When your site is open to the public, stand inside, just off to the side of the main entrance. Watch people coming in. Notice how they look around, what catches their attention, and what they ignore. You'll see the point at which they make the adjustment and are "in." That point is where your transition zone ends.

- If the zone is too big (meaning visitors are missing too much), brainstorm ways to shorten the zone. Place signs, welcome desks, or reading material out of the transition zone. Put these where visitors are able to take them in after they have made their transition to your space.

- Train all staff members to keep the transition zone clear and to wait to approach visitors until after they're "in."

Exercise 9B:
Making the most of the right-hand bias

- The right front corner of your site is prime real estate and should house something of key importance. If you can, create traffic flow patterns that take advantage of this right-hand bias. (In the UK and other countries where driving is done on the left, the bias toward the right is less pronounced.)

- When you're renovating or building a new site, use the right-hand bias to showcase important items and help manage traffic flow.

Exercise 9C:
Reviewing your map

- Review your target-visitor boards (from Exercise 5C) while looking at your map. "Busy" maps should be reworked to focus on details of interest to your target visitors. Key elements like food and bathrooms should be easy to locate. Include items only if they add to your target visitors' experience, not because a department head wants to promote something.

- If you're redesigning your map, choose a graphic designer with experience in "You Are Here" maps. Have him create the map with an isometric (also called axonometric or oblique) perspective, rather than a plan view.

- Creating the art in "layers" in a graphic design program allows items to be easily updated. Ask your designer to provide art for your redesigned map art on files compatible with your software, so you can make simple updates yourself. And have the designer produce a version of the map suitable for your Web site.

- Large sites need "You Are Here" maps printed in large format. Ask your front-line staff to identify places where visitors ask for directions. Put maps at those major decision-making points. Orient every "You Are Here" map to its unique location; "up" on the map is the direction the viewer is facing. Protect the "You Are Here" symbol with Plexiglas or make it of raised bronze.

- Test new maps with visitors using inexpensive prototype versions in place. Watch visitors using the maps, and ask if they're working.

Exercise 9D:

Rate your wayfinding system

- Front-line staff can tell you if your wayfinding system is working properly. You might approach visitors with "We've had some complaints from people who couldn't find their way around. Was there anything you think might be confusing to someone else?" Or, "Was there anything you couldn't find that you were looking for?" Questions like these elicit useful feedback.

- To create a wayfinding system, you'll need a map of your site on a clipboard, a pencil, some small rectangular sticky notes, and some sticky arrow tags. Walk your site and put a numbered arrow tag at each location on the map where a sign is needed. Consider important decision-making points and locations where views are blocked. Draw a mini-version of each sign on a sticky note, including directional arrows and a number matching its location.

- Good wayfinding systems divide a site into five to seven regions and use different colors and icons to distinguish each region.

- Print temporary mockups of each sign and place them in the proposed locations, testing them with first-time visitors. You may find you need fewer signs, or that your placement is off, or that wording needs to change. If you install a new system, **take down all the old wayfinding signs.**

- Review the placement and condition of all your signs regularly, as temporary and obsolete signs have a way of mysteriously proliferating.

Exercise 9E:

How's your placement?

- Test the placement of signs, exhibits, or display elements by watching how visitors interact with them. Watch for the "butt brush effect"; make sure signs aren't blocked when it's crowded.

- In queue areas, place short signs, flyers, or other displays **within reach**. Longer signs or video monitors can go in longer lines.

Chapter 10 Summary

- Make people comfortable by meeting their basic physical needs; it increases their stay time. They'll spend more time, attention, and money with you and will learn more.

- Invest in comfortable seating. Use visitor feedback to help you place or upgrade your seating.

- Clean, well-maintained restrooms are key comfort zones. Use painted finishes, lighting, and scented lotions and soaps to create a pleasant atmosphere. Keep children, strollers, and wheelchair users in mind when you're designing new restrooms.

- When you can provide it, serve food themed to your experience. It's a great way to increase revenue and stay time, while making visitors comfortable.

- When you're planning exhibit components, labels, or interactive touch screens, make sure the effort needed to understand the information isn't more than the reward provided by the sign or screen.

- People feel more psychological comfort when they can find their way around, feel safe, and see that facilities are clean. Budget for and schedule regular maintenance. Don't build anything you can't afford to maintain.

Further reading for Chapter 10

- Lisa Brochu, *Interpretive Planning: The 5-M Model for Successful Planning Projects* (available through www.interpnet.com).

  Chapter 8—"Mechanics"—details the mechanics of creating comfort; the author's real-world experience can be applied to a variety of sites.

- Disney Institute, *Be Our Guest: Perfecting the Art of Customer Service*.

  Chapter 4—"The Magic of Setting"— explains how the details of a setting create a service environment.

- John H. Falk and Lynn D. Dierking, *Learning from Museums: Visitor Experiences and the Making of Meaning*.

  Chapter 4—"The Physical Context"— shows how physical comfort enhances learning, supporting nonprofit missions.

- Malcolm Gladwell, *The Tipping Point: How Little Things Make a Big Difference*.

  Chapter 4—Part one: "The Power of Context"—explores how setting creates (or discourages) crime; more on the broken-window theory.

- Rachel Kaplan, Stephen Kaplan, and Robert L. Ryan, *With People in Mind: Design and Management of Everyday Nature*.

  Chapter 3—"Fears and Preferences"— demonstrates how visitors' discomfort shortens stay time at parks, keeping people from fully exploring the sites' offerings.

Exercise 10A:
"Body comfort" review

- Revisit your **restrooms** to see if they reflect the highest level of comfort you can provide. Be sure they are clean, in good working order, and well stocked. Replace dripping, cracked, or leaky fixtures. Brainstorm with your team how your restrooms could better relay your organization's personality and theme and meet the needs of your target visitors.

- The type of organization you have and the size of your site will determine how much **seating** you need and what kind it should be. If you are making a major purchase, try out samples of benches and chairs before you buy to be certain they're comfortable.

- If you already offer **food**, does it need an upgrade? Does it match your theme and suit your target visitors? If you don't offer food, is there food close by?

- Have some moms or dads bring their kids in **double strollers** to test how comfortable it is to maneuver around your site. Invite people who use **wheelchairs or walkers** as well. They'll give you instant feedback. This is especially valuable if you are in the early planning stages of a renovation or expansion. Your visitor "consultants" will notice things you won't.

Exercise 10B:
"Mind comfort" review

- How **safe** is your space? Check for sharp edges, places kids can bump their heads, and other unsafe aspects. How is the lighting? Do any dim hallways need brightening up? If your parking lot or garage doesn't feel safe, get together with other tenants and the garage owners to organize a plan to improve it.

- Take a look at your **signs** and other media like touch screens. Are they easy to read and easy to understand? Ask someone who is over forty-five, and someone over sixty, to read them as well. Our eyes yellow as we get older, so we need more light, larger type, and higher contrast.

Exercise 10C:
Maintenance

- Look at your site's **dirt factor**. Check wear and tear on the carpeting, flooring, front door, information desk, store counters, and dressing rooms if you have them. Check places that visitors spend a lot of time touching, like keyboards. If surfaces aren't wearing well, consider upgrading materials when you replace the items.

- Establish a regular maintenance plan, and assign one person or department to manage it. A maintenance plan should include a budget, a site inspection, and a listing of projects. Consider these categories: painting, carpeting/flooring, railings and stairs, fixtures or exhibit components, seating, signage, plumbing, and heating/cooling. Prioritize the projects based on 1) visitor safety, 2) compliance with regulations regarding disability access, 3) functionality, 4) esthetics/first impression.

Chapter 11 Summary

- Create a one-sentence theme for your organization that supports your experience and guides your visitor communication.

- Good themes touch on universal concepts like love, loyalty, and honor.

- Use an action verb in the theme sentence; the sentence answers the question "Why should I care?"

- Create in-house guidelines for written communication at your site. Specify tone, voice, length, size and styles of typeface, and languages.

- Guidelines for spoken communication might include telephone scripts for training and examples of proper ways for staff members to speak and act when they're "onstage" with visitors.

Further reading for Chapter 11

- Larry Beck and Ted T. Cable, *Interpretation for the 21st Century: Fifteen Guiding Principles for Interpreting Nature and Culture.*

  Chapter 10—"Tenth Principle: Technique Before Art"

  Chapter 11—"Eleventh Principle: Interpretive Composition"

  For quality interpretive speaking and writing.

- Mary Kay Cunningham, *The Interpreters Training Manual for Museums.*

  A self-contained training manual by the founder of Visitor Dialogue.

- Disney Institute, *Be Our Guest: Perfecting the Art of Customer Service.*

  Chapter 2—"The Magic of Service"

  Chapter 3—"The Magic of the Cast"

  The masters of the art give specifics on improving customer communication.

- Seth Godin, *All Marketers Are Liars: The Power of Telling Authentic Stories in a Low-Trust World.*

  Invaluable ideas on customer communication.

- T. Scott Gross, *Outrageous! Unforgettable Service . . . Guilt-free Selling.*

  Chapter 13—"Things Servers Have to Know"—chock full of tips.

- Beverly Serrell, *Exhibit Labels: An Interpretive Approach.*

  This is the signage bible, featuring Serrell's "Big Idea."

Exercise 11A:
Creating your theme

- This exercise takes place over two days. It's helpful if you recap your mission, target audience(s), and brand personality and post them on the wall before you begin. Your goal is to write a single theme sentence. Tape up five large sheets of paper or divide a large dry-erase board into five sections. Label them from left to right: "subject," "action verb," "consequence," "universal themes." Leave the fifth sheet or section of the board blank.

- Start with your **subject**. List all the possible subjects for your organizational theme. You could focus on the subject of your collection, the service you provide, the kind of experience you offer, or your visitors themselves. Avoid vague terms like "we," "them," or "our visitors." When you've listed every possibility, move on to the outcome. (Leave the action verb section blank for now.)

- The **outcome** is the answer to the question "What does this mean to me?" or "Why should I care?" List all the possible ideas for your outcome, using the list from the subject section for inspiration.

  Example: If you run a children's museum and you listed "families" as a possible subject for your theme, then the list of outcomes might include togetherness, affordable leisure time, trying new things, or offering healthy activities.

- Now you'll work on your **action verb**. Avoid "is," "are," "transforms," "impacts," or "represents." Be more specific. Make a list of possible verbs. The verb should link some of your best ideas for subjects with their outcomes.

  Example: In a children's museum, families could: "enjoy," "explore," "relax," or "learn about" some of the outcomes listed above.

- To fill in the fourth section, choose any of these positive **universal themes** that apply to your organization (or add your own): loyalty, love, morality, independence, tolerance, power, transformation, dedication, life and death.

- It's best at this point to take a break for a day to let these ideas percolate. Invite everyone on the team to come back with a suggestion for a theme sentence.

- When you reconvene, ask people to share their thoughts about the previous day's discussion. Go through each section, circling the one or two suggestions in each column that the team feels are strongest and that fit your organization best.

- If people have offered up theme sentences for consideration, write these in the fifth section, then work with their suggestions and those circled words to craft a theme sentence for your organization.

- If you get stuck as a group, assign one person with the best writing skills to fine-tune the sentence to distill the essence of your discussion.

- Your theme sentence might describe your organization better than your mission statement; you can revise your mission statement now. Include your new theme in all your internal documents, your

Experience*ology* binder, and your employee handbook. Use it for all types of planning. In addition, you might want to craft a theme-based tag line for your advertising, business cards, and other printed materials.

Exercise 11B:
Guidelines for written communication

- Get out and look at all the signs posted at your site, and take photos of the different styles. You may have just a few signs; a large outdoor park or zoo may have hundreds. Note any inconsistencies in the writing style or visual design as you go. It will help to have someone new to your staff work on this project; they'll have a fresh point of view.

- Write up guidelines for new signs and include them in your Experience*ology* binder. The length of your guidelines will depend on the number of signs you have. For a few signs you'll need just a short page of guidelines. If you have a very complex signage system you will need to develop a signage manual. Your guidelines should include instructions about the tone and voice of your writing, grade level and readability goals, ideal length of copy for different types of signs, typeface(s) to be used, and any notes about design, size, materials, production, and cost that are important to include. Thorough guidelines will help a newcomer or consultant produce signs that match the rest of your themed experience.

- Consider creating a fictional character or spokesperson to be the voice of your organization.

- *Note: While this book is targeted to sites where English is the primary language, the principles apply anywhere.*

- How will you communicate with non-English speakers who are part of your target audience(s)? Think about your signs, flyers, or brochures. Do you need to publish these in multiple languages? If you have staff members who are bilingual, make sure you let your visitors know it. If your target visitors speak a language other than English, hire people who speak that language when you're adding staff.

Exercise 11C:
Guidelines for spoken communication

- Discuss with your team how staff members should answer the phone, respond to visitors' questions and problems, and speak when "onstage." Write up some simple, clear guidelines for everyone to follow. These are especially important for training new staff members.

- If your site has educational content, provide interpretive training for all front-line staff, paid or unpaid. Mary Kay Cunningham's book *The Interpreters Training Manual for Museums* is an excellent self-contained resource.

Chapter 12 Summary

- Fun is an important part of a dynamic workplace. Your staff members should be having fun and playing with visitors, as appropriate, to make your experience come alive.

- Sensation represents one of the three contexts for informal learning, meshing with the physical and intellectual contexts. Design spaces that encourage conversation and group activities to stimulate learning.

- Engage all five senses whenever possible. Provide full-body experiences and let visitors smell, touch, taste, and hear your exhibits, or any products you sell.

- Stage unexpected, random, and out-of-proportion surprises for maximum impact on your visitors.

Further reading for Chapter 12

- Disney Institute, *Be Our Guest: Perfecting the Art of Customer Service.*

  Chapter 4—"The Magic of Setting"—provides quick reference factoids on the five senses.

- John H. Falk and Lynn D. Dierking, *Lessons Without Limit: How Free-Choice Learning Is Transforming Education.*

  Chapter 12—"The Free-Choice Learner's Bill of Rights"—makes recommendations for creating environments that facilitate learning through sensory experiences.

- T. Scott Gross, *Positively Outrageous Service: How to Delight and Astound Your Customers and Win Them for Life.*

  Chapter 6—"Finding Opportunities to Serve Outrageously"—details ways to add fun to every aspect of your customer service.

- B. Joseph Pine II and James H. Gilmore, *The Experience Economy: Work Is Theatre & Every Business a Stage.*

  Chapter 6—"Work Is Theatre"—shows you how to use theater techniques to enrich your experience on a daily basis.

- Paco Underhill, *Why We Buy: The Science of Shopping.*

  Chapter 12—"The Sensual Shopper"—provides guidelines for maximizing the sensory aspects of shopping.

- For additional resources on sensation, visit www.experienceology.com.

Exercise 12A:
The Ad Hoc Silly Committee

- To create fun for your staff, put together a team of people who like to laugh and play. Assign them the task of keeping staff morale high. Support their efforts by providing some funds if needed and the time required to execute special secret jobs. Don't monitor them too closely. Nothing kills fun faster than rules, guidelines, or having to report back regularly. (It goes without saying that you can trust them. You should trust *all* your staff members.)

Exercise 12B:
The five senses review

- Look for fingerprints, carpet wear patterns, scuffing, and furniture that's been rearranged. Those are all clues that people are using their senses to experience your space. Rather than trying to discourage it, analyze what is happening to see how you can enhance the experience while minimizing maintenance. For example, if kids regularly run their hands along a painted wall, making it a constant challenge to keep clean, install a strip of bumpy plastic as a visual "chair rail" that will hide the fingerprints while giving little fingers a tactile jolt.

- Have your team review your site. Brainstorm ways to add:
  Unusual visuals
  Sounds and music
  Tastes and sips
  Scents and smells
  Touch and textures

Exercise 12C:
Upping the fun factor

- Develop a plan for creating repeatable surprises. This can include drop-in activities like unscheduled tours, tastings, sniffings, or hands-on art activities. If you have a budget for advertising and promotion, consider diverting some of it to create surprises for visitors. You can target members with a higher lifetime value (see Chapter 4) and choose surprises that will create a lot of positive word of mouth.

Chapter 13 Summary

- Top businesses make it a point to constantly ask, "Can we do better?" Strong, healthy organizations value and welcome critical voices from staff members at every level.

- Follow trend-watching Web sites to get new ideas for your business and to stay relevant to your visitors. Try www.trendwatching.com to get started.

- It's important to ask your visitors what they want and then try to give it to them, rather than assuming that they want what you're offering. One of your communication goals is to hear back from your visitors and shape your offerings in response to their requests and feedback.

- Use the information you get from your visitors to shape the price of your products, programs, and admission as well as the hours you are open.

- Consider creating new partnerships with all kinds of other businesses and organizations to strengthen your experience and fulfill your organizational mission.

Further reading for Chapter 13

- Stephen T. Asma, *Stuffed Animals and Pickled Heads: The Culture and Evolution of Natural History Museums.* Chapter 6—"Evolution and the Roulette Wheel: A Chance Cosmos Rattles Some Bones"—a fascinating insider's look at evaluation.

- Chip Bell and Bilijack Bell, *Magnetic Service: Secrets for Creating Passionately Devoted Customers.* Secret #2—"Focus on Customer Hopes, Not Just Needs"—details clever ways to assess what customers might want.

- Lisa Brochu, *Interpretive Planning: The 5-M Model for Successful Planning Projects.* Chapter 6—"Markets"—real-world advice on price, placement, and assessing markets.

- David F. D'Alessandro, *Brand Warfare: 10 Rules for Building the Killer Brand.* Rule 6—"Do Not Confuse Sponsorship with a Spectator Sport"—discusses corporate sponsorship from the other side of the table.

- Judy Diamond, *Practical Evaluation Guide: Tools for Museums & Other Informal Educational Settings.* Everything you ever wanted to know about visitor studies.

- Marc Gobé, *Citizen Brand: 10 Commandments for Transforming Brands in a Consumer Democracy.* Chapter 1—"The First Commandment: Evolve From Consumers to People"—a rich analysis of trends and markets.

Exercise 13A:
Common-sense scorecard

- Place three large pieces of paper on the wall and label them "operational common sense," "cultural common sense," and "alignment common sense." Invite all your employees to post their thoughts on ways to improve your business practices in each area. How can you improve or streamline your operations? How can you better reflect diverse cultures? Are your business practices always in line with your mission?

- After a week, sit down with your team and prioritize each list, assigning a work group or individual to move forward on high-priority items. Have the team or staff member report back monthly.

Exercise 13B:
Gold mine on the front line

- If your site is small, you are all front-line staff members. If you have a large staff, you'll have to work harder to collect input from your front line. If some staff wear uniforms and some don't, be aware that you have an internal gap to bridge (even if you think everyone gets along well). Uniformed staff members are always front-line and may be members of a union. Don't assume that they will buy into changes just because you announce them. You will have to convince them that you care about their input.

- Decide on the best ways to collect front-line information. This could include (paid) brainstorming sessions, suggestion boxes or submission areas on your employee intranet

(with a monthly reward like a gift certificate), and a temporary committee set up to develop new ideas from the front line.

- Type up the plan, including who will be responsible for implementing it. Include it in your Experience*ology* binder (described on page 139).

Exercise 13C:
Trend watch

- Check out www.trendwatching.com and www.nowandnext.com. Find three trends relevant to your business, then discuss and brainstorm about them with your staff. At least one person at your site should subscribe to these e-newsletters to keep in touch with new trends.

Exercise 13D:
Ask the audience

- At this point in the process you might be ready to do more in-depth research with your visitors. First decide whether you need to use informal or formal means.

- **Informal** surveys: Set up a logbook for front-line staff to use for noting damage, wear and tear, and other signs of visitor use. Once a month, run a density check: have a staff person go through your site every hour, marking Xs on a map of your site where each visitor is standing. Encourage front-line staff members to ask visitors for feedback. Some starter questions are: "We've received some complaints about X. What do you think?" "Was there anything you *didn't* find that you were looking for/expecting?" "Is there one thing we could change that would make our site better for you?" These questions give visitors permission to give you negative feedback.

- **Formal** surveys: Pick up a copy of Judy Diamond's *Practical Evaluation Guide: Tools for Museums & Other Informal Educational Settings* to help you decide what kinds of surveys to use and how to go about collecting more in-depth information.

- Use a questionnaire or interview to ask visitors about your prices, hours, new exhibits, and programs. Review the Diamond book for information on how to craft your questions to collect this information.

- You may only be doing push communication now—sending out information about your offerings, hoping the information is reaching visitors interested in what you offer. If this describes you, it's time to consider doing some pull communication. To get started, look into technologies like blogs, podcasts, and discussion boards to get visitors engaged in your business.

Exercise 13E:
Creative partnerships

- On a large sheet of paper or dry-erase board make three columns: "like-minded organizations," "larger companies," and "parallel businesses" (see pages 121–23). In each column list at least five names that might provide some kind of partnership opportunity. These could include money, in-kind donations, co-marketing, providing

services, or creating new products, programs, or services that would benefit both of you.

- Choose the most promising name from each category and assign someone to follow up on that idea, with a one-month deadline for reporting back.

Chapter 14 Summary

- The way you end your experience is as important as the way you begin it. Consider the "last impression" you make on visitors when you design your finale. That take-home impression will lead to positive word-of-mouth advertising and the desire to come back.

- A key part of the finale is to invite your visitors to come back, to become members, or to sign up for another class. If you don't ask, you may miss the opportunity to serve them again.

- Make sure any materials your visitors take home communicate your brand, are equal in quality to the rest of your experience, and encourage people to visit you again.

- Souvenirs fall into five categories: "Images," "Pieces-of-the-rock," "Local products," "Markers," and "Symbolic shorthand."

- Mementos and memorabilia are an important part of all crafted experiences. Make sure yours can stand alone to tell your brand story after they leave your site. Every piece associated with your organization should be high quality and worth saving.

Further reading for Chapter 14

- John H. Falk and Lynn D. Dierking, *The Museum Experience.*

  Chapter 6—"The Interplay of Contexts: The Museum as Gestalt"—guides you in thinking through every aspect of the museum experience in a fresh way.

- Marc Gobé, *Citizen Brand: 10 Commandments for Transforming Brands in a Consumer Democracy.*

  Chapter 3—"The Third Commandment: Evolve From Product to Experience"— gives compelling descriptions of branded environments.

- Tom Kelley, *The Art of Innovation: Lessons in Creativity from IDEO, America's Leading Design Firm.*

  Chapter 10—"Creating Experiences for Fun and Profit"—breaks down the DNA of experiences.

- Tim Merriman and Lisa Brochu, *Management of Interpretive Sites: Developing Sustainable Operations through Effective Leadership.*

  Chapter 8—"Memorabilia"— details suggestions for high-quality gift-shop offerings.

- For additional finale resources, visit www.experienceology.com.

Exercise 14A:

Ending with a whimper or a bang?

- Stand near your exit and watch people leave. What is their last impression? Who is saying goodbye to them? Are there any signs or graphics that effectively talk to visitors as they leave?

- Think about what you are saying to visitors as they exit. Develop a farewell script for this occasion. Thank people for coming, invite them to come back, ask them for referrals, and, if you have memberships, suggest that they join.

Exercise 14B:

Your take-home materials become mementos

- Collect an example of *anything* that goes home with visitors, including cash-register or other receipts, ticket stubs, tissue, bags, boxes, handouts, brochures, and maps. Do they reflect your theme and brand look? What is missing? Is anything you give away worth saving as a memento? Can you improve the quality to make it worth keeping? Is everything immediately identifiable as yours?

- If you decide to use loyalty cards ("Buy 10, Get 1 Free") at your coffee kiosk or shop, you can offer to store them for visitors as a courtesy. This allows you to interact with them during their checkout and provides a nice service as well. If you date the cards when they are punched, it gives you an easy way to gauge the frequency of people's visits.

Exercise 14C:

Memorabilia for sale

- Divide a large piece of paper or dry-erase board into six columns. Label them "Images," "Pieces-of-the-rock," "Local products," "Markers," "Symbolic shorthand," and "other." Write down everything you currently sell or give away, putting each item into one of these categories. Is one column very light, while others are full? Keep in mind that your visitors are less likely to keep markers and symbolic shorthand. If an item doesn't seem to fit any of the categories, put it in "other." The longer people keep an item, the stronger a connection they make to you. Ask yourself: Is it worth saving for a lifetime? Does it further our mission? Brainstorm ideas for developing merchandise for the first three categories that conveys your theme.

- Choose memorabilia that beautifully reflects your experience. Everything you sell should be high quality and provide a wide range of price points.

Congratulations!

- You have now completed the review of your site and should be well on your way as an experience-based business. Be sure to visit experienceology.com regularly to share ideas and find new resources.

NOTES

The following sources, frequently cited, are referred to in abbreviated form:

All Marketers Are Liars

Seth Godin, *All Marketers Are Liars: The Power of Telling Authentic Stories in a Low-Trust World* (New York: Portfolio, 2005).

Be Our Guest

Disney Institute, *Be Our Guest: Perfecting the Art of Customer Service* (New York: Disney Editions, 2001).

Branded Nation

James B. Twitchell, *Branded Nation: The Marketing of Megachurch, College Inc., and Museumworld* (New York: Simon and Schuster, 2004).

Built to Last

Jim Collins and Jerry I. Porras, *Built to Last: Successful Habits of Visionary Companies* (New York: HarperBusiness, 1994).

Call of the Mall

Paco Underhill, *The Call of the Mall: The Geography of Shopping* (New York: Simon and Schuster, 2004).

Citizen Brand

Marc Gobé, *Citizen Brand: 10 Commandments for Transforming Brands in a Consumer Democracy* (New York: Allworth Press, 2002).

Emotional Branding

Marc Gobé, *Emotional Branding: The New Paradigm for Connecting Brands to People* (New York: Allworth Press, 2001).

Experience Economy

B. Joseph Pine II and James H. Gilmore, *The Experience Economy: Work Is Theatre & Every Business a Stage* (Boston: Harvard Business School Press, 1999).

Fabled Service

Betsy Sanders, *Fabled Service: Ordinary Acts, Extraordinary Outcomes* (San Diego: Pfeiffer and Company, 1995).

Guts!

Kevin Freiberg and Jackie Freiberg, *Guts!: Companies That Blow the Doors Off Business-as-Usual* (New York: Doubleday, 2004).

Learning from Museums

John H. Falk and Lynn D. Dierking, *Learning from Museums: Visitor Experiences and the Making of Meaning* (Walnut Creek, Calif.: AltaMira Press, 2000).

Museum Experience

John H. Falk and Lynn D. Dierking, *The Museum Experience* (Washington, D.C.: Whalesback Books, 1992).

Nuts!

Kevin Freiberg and Jackie Freiberg, *Nuts! Southwest Airlines' Crazy Recipe for Personal and Business Success* (Austin, Tex.: Bard Press, 1996).

Psychology of the Consumer

Robert C. Webb, *Psychology of the Consumer and Its Development: An Introduction* (New York: Kluwer Academic-Plenum Publishers, 1999).

Why We Buy

Paco Underhill, *Why We Buy: The Science of Shopping* (New York: Simon and Schuster, 1999).

With People in Mind

Rachel Kaplan, Stephen Kaplan, and Robert L. Ryan, *With People in Mind: Design and Management of Everyday Nature* (Washington, D.C.: Island Press, 1998).

Chapter 1

1. *Experience Economy*
2. *Museum Experience*
3. Bill Capodagli and Lynn Jackson, *The Disney Way: Harnessing the Management Secrets of Disney in Your Company* (New York: McGraw Hill, 1999). Holding on to just five percent of your visitors increases your profitability by twenty-five to a hundred percent.
4. Ibid.
5. Cia Romano, principal, Interface Guru, telephone conversation with the author, August 3, 2005.
6. Richard Louv, *Last Child in the Woods: Saving Our Children from Nature-Deficit Disorder* (Chapel Hill, N.C.: Algonquin Books, 2005).
7. *Experience Economy* (see page 189)
8. *Why We Buy* (see page 189)
9. David Lewis and Darren Bridger, *The Soul of the New Consumer* (London: Nicholas Brealey Publishing, 2000). A phenomenal success story, Starbucks is also discussed in *Experience Economy* and *Emotional Branding*.
10. *Experience Economy*
11. *Be Our Guest*
12. *All Marketers Are Liars*
13. Robert Spector and Patrick D. McCarthy, *The Nordstrom Way: The Inside Story of America's #1 Customer Service Company* (New York: John Wiley and Sons, 2000). Nordstrom's custom seating is also mentioned in *Emotional Branding*.
14. *Nuts!* Southwest Airlines' deliberately casual uniforms are covered in the Costume section of *Experience Economy*.
15. Reinier Evers, "Being Spaces & Brand Spaces," *Trend Briefing*, March 2006; www.trendwatching.com.
16. Ibid.
17. Lisa Brochu, *Interpretive Planning: The 5-M Model for Successful Planning Projects* (Fort Collins, Colo.: Interp Press, 2003).
18. The debate continues in the museum field. See Terri Castaneda, "Come to the Dark Side . . . What Is Authenticity in Museums?" *WestMuse* (Fall 2005). In her presentation at the annual meeting of the Western Museums Association, Castaneda discussed the challenges of maintaining authenticity in the midst of competition and market pressures, including those that come from within an institution.
19. "In Brief," *Museum News*, July–August 2004. Zagat rates sites on such factors as adult and child appeal, facilities, and service. Museums even have competition from each other. According to James B. Twitchell in *Branded Nation*, there are at least eleven thousand museums in the U.S. Twenty new museum projects are under construction in Washington, D. C. alone (quoted in Martha Morris, "Expansionism . . . Successes and Failures," *Museum News*, July–August 2004).
20. DeNeen Brown, "Washington's Museums: Worth the Price of Admission?" www.washingtonpost.com, April 13, 2006.
21. *Branded Nation*. If you think an art museum is aiming at a different audience than a Coke museum, the High Museum's Web site describes it as a "tourism destination and entertainment attraction"; when I viewed the home page it featured a jazz music series and kids' art activities; www.high.org.
22. Amanda Litvinov, "Chronicles," *Museum News*, March-April 2006.
23. Cia Romano, principal, Interface Guru, telephone conversation with the author, August 3, 2005.
24. D. Keith Denton and Charles Boyd, *Did You Know? Fascinating Facts and Fallacies about Business* (Upper Saddle River, N.J.: Prentice Hall, 1994), quoted in *Fabled Service*.
25. Capodagli and Jackson, *Disney Way*.

Chapter 2

1. *Experience Economy*
2. *Why We Buy*
3. *Built to Last*
4. Lisa Brochu, *Interpretive Planning: The 5-M Model for Successful Planning Projects* (Fort Collins, Colo.: Interp Press, 2003).
5. Rolf Jensen, *The Dream Society: How the Coming Shift from Information to Imagination Will Transform Your Business* (New York: McGraw Hill, 1999).
6. Brochu, *Interpretive Planning*.
7. Web site of the Texas State Aquarium, Corpus Christi: www.texasstateaquarium.org.

Chapter 3

1. United States Department of Labor, Bureau of Labor Statistics, "Time-Use Survey," USDL 04-1797. www.bls.gov/tus/note01122005.htm. John P. Robinson and Geoffrey Godbey, *Time for Life: The Surprising Ways Americans Use Their Time* (University Park, Pa.: The Pennsylvania State University Press, 1997).

2. Ellen Wulfhorst, "Americans Commute Longer, Farther than Ever," *San Diego Union-Tribune*, April 22, 2006.

3. Kristin Friedrich, "Midnight at the Museum," www.losangelesdowntownnews.com, August 4, 2005.

4. The regular attendees made up a mere fourteen percent of Toledo's population during Hood's 1980-81 study. She recommended the museum make the facility more comfortable and welcoming. She encouraged the museum to offer more programs with active participation and social interaction to draw people who'd been visiting only occasionally and those who would ordinarily be non-attendees. The museum added comfortable seating in the lobby and a welcoming information office, and they changed their programming mix as well. Consultant Judy Rand believes that museums have an obligation to see things from visitors' perspective. To honor their role in the relationship, she developed "A Visitor's Bill of Rights," suggesting that visitors have choices about where to go and what to do and deserve to leave feeling refreshed. Beverly Serrell adds that excellent museum exhibits should be both engaging and meaningful. Marilyn Hood, "Staying Away: Why People Choose Not to Visit Museums," in *Reinventing the Museum: Historical and Contemporary Perspectives on the Paradigm Shift*, ed. Gail Anderson (Walnut Creek, Calif.: AltaMira Press, 2004; first published in *Museum News*, April 1983). Judy Rand, "A Visitor's Bill of Rights," in Anderson, ed., *Reinventing the Museum* (first published in *Curator: The Museum Journal* 44, no. 1, January 2000). Beverly Serrell, *Judging Exhibitions: A Framework for Assessing Excellence* (Walnut Creek, Calif.: Left Coast Press, 2006).

5. Francie Ostrower, *Motivations Matter: Findings and Practical Implications of a National Survey of Cultural Participation* (n.p.: The Urban Institute and The Wallace Foundation, 2005); www.urban.org or www.wallacefoundation.org.

6. *The Experience Economy*

7. en.wikipedia.org/wiki/Cerritos_Millenium_Library.

8. Eric I. Arnold, Linda L. Price, and Patrick Tierney, "The Wilderness Servicescape: An Ironic Commercial Landscape," in *ServiceScapes: The Concept of Place in Contemporary Markets*, ed. John F. Sherry, Jr. (Chicago: NTC Business Books, 1998).

9. www.neofuturists.org.

10. Mary Sue Novy, office manager, Jungle Roots Children's Dentistry, Chandler, Ariz., interview with the author, March 20, 2006.

11. *Citizen Brand*

12. David Lewis and Darren Bridger, *The Soul of the New Consumer* (London: Nicholas Brealey Publishing, 2000).

13. Russell W. Belk, "The Role of Possessions in Constructing and Maintaining a Sense of Past," *Advances in Consumer Research* 17 (1990).

14. Russell W. Belk, "Possessions and the Sense of Past," in *Highways and Buyways: Naturalistic Research from the Consumer Behavior Odyssey*, ed. Russell W. Belk (Provo, Utah: Association for Consumer Research, 1991).

15. Russell W. Belk, Melanie Wallendorf, and John F. Sherry, Jr., "The Sacred and the Profane in Consumer Behavior: Theodicy on the Odyssey," *Journal of Consumer Research* 16 (June 1989).

16. Roberta Colombo Dougoud, "Souvenirs from Kambot (Papua New Guinea): The Sacred Search for Authenticity," in *Souvenirs: The Material Culture of Tourism*, eds. Michael Hitchcock and Ken Teague (Aldershot, UK: Ashgate Publishing, 2000).

17. Jennifer Scarce, "Tourism and Material Culture in Turkey," in *Souvenirs: The Material Culture of Tourism*, Hitchcock and Teague, eds.

18. Joseph Pine and James Gilmore, *Pine & Gilmore's Field Guide for the Experience Economy* (Aurora, Ohio: Strategic Horizons, 2005).

19. *All Marketers Are Liars*

20. Lewis and Bridger, *Soul of the New Consumer*.

21. Ray Oldenburg, *The Great Good Place: Cafes, Coffee Shops, Bookstores, Bars, Hair Salons, and Other Hangouts at the Heart of Community* (New York: Marlowe and Company, 1999).

22. Can museums become third places for at least some of their community members? Yes, if they rethink the way they do business. Museum consultants Harold and Susan Skramstad see the "ideal museum" as a community of choice for large numbers of people in the future. "Dreaming the Museum," *Museum News*, March–April 2005.

23. Reinier Evers, "Being Spaces & Brand Spaces," *Trend Briefing*, March 2006; www.trendwatching.com.

24. Frank Green, "More Malls Cozying Up to Visitors: Stores Hope Shoppers Will Feel at Home, Spend More," *San Diego Union-Tribune*, April 26, 2006.

25. Evers, "Being Spaces."

26. *Psychology of the Consumer*

Chapter 4

1. My thanks to the hundreds of behaviorists (many of whose research I have condensed) for their dedicated work. I am especially indebted to Professor Robert C. Webb, whose paper, "The Relevance of the Consumer Research Literature to the Visitor Studies Field: The Case of Involvement," given at the 1993 Visitor Studies Association conference, planted the seed for my exploration of the connection between museums and retail.

2. James O. Prochaska, John C. Norcross, and Carlo C. DiClemente, *Changing for Good: A Revolutionary Six-Stage Program for Overcoming Bad Habits and Moving Your Life Positively Forward* (New York: William Morrow, 1994). All of the information about the six stages of behavior change is from this well-researched and helpful book.

3. *Psychology of the Consumer*

4. *Why We Buy*

5. *Psychology of the Consumer*

6. Malcolm Gladwell, *The Tipping Point: How Little Things Make a Big Difference* (Boston: Little, Brown and Company, 2000).

7. Melissa Bateson, Daniel Nettle, and Gilbert Roberts, "Cues of Being Watched Enhance Cooperation in a Real-World Setting," *Biology Letters* (doi:10.1098/rsbl.2006.0509; published online).

8. John H. Falk and Beverly K. Sheppard, *Thriving in the Knowledge Age: New Business Models for Museums and Other Cultural Institutions* (Lanham, Md.: AltaMira Press, 2006).

9. Don Peppers and Martha Rogers, *Enterprise One to One: Tools for Competing in the Interactive Age* (New York: Currency Books, 1997).

10. Francie Ostrower, *Motivations Matter: Findings and Practical Implications of a National Survey of Cultural Participation* (n.p.: The Urban Institute and The Wallace Foundation, 2005); www.urban.org or www.wallacefoundation.org.

11. *Call of the Mall*

12. Frank Green, "More Malls Cozying Up to Visitors: Stores Hope Shoppers Will Feel at Home, Spend More," *San Diego Union-Tribune*, April 26, 2006. Average spending for thirty-to-sixty-minute stays: $67.30; average spending for two to three hours: $140.20.

13. Larry Beck, "'Wicked' Interpretation: Lessons from Broadway," *The Interpreter* 1, no. 4 (July-August

2005). Some sites have incredible duration figures. At Gettysburg National Military Park, the average stay is eight hours, with only eighteen percent of the visitors staying for fewer than four hours. John Gatewood and Catherine Cameron, "Battlefield Pilgrims at Gettysburg National Military Park," *Ethnology* 43, no. 3 (Summer 2004).

14. I include docents and other volunteers in this group.

15. John H. Falk and Lynn D. Dierking, *Lessons Without Limit: How Free-Choice Learning Is Transforming Education* (Walnut Creek, Calif.: AltaMira Press, 2002).

16. *Why We Buy*

17. If you enjoy consumer psychology, you'll be interested to learn that positive word-of-mouth advertising is actually a form of vicarious operant conditioning. That is, we do things because we have heard or seen others rewarded for that behavior (*Psychology of the Consumer*).

18. This is also called social marketing. See Kris Whipple's excellent article "From Intention to Action: Inspiring Behavior Change," *The Interpreter* 1, no. 6 (November-December 2005).

19. For two examples, visit www.mbayaq.org and www.brookfieldzoo.org.

Chapter 5

1. David F. D'Alessandro, *Brand Warfare: 10 Rules for Building the Killer Brand* (New York: McGraw Hill, 2001).

2. Karen Beery, district interpretive coordinator, California State Parks, e-mail communication with the author, December 14, 2005.

3. Naomi Klein, *No Logo: Taking Aim at the Brand Bullies* (New York: Picador USA, 1999).

4. Duane Knapp and Gary Sherwin, *Destination BrandScience* (Washington, D.C.,: International Association of Convention and Visitors Bureaus, 2005).

5. Sean Adams and Noreen Morioka, *Logo Design Workbook: A Hands-on Guide to Creating Logos* (Gloucester, Mass.: Rockport Publishers, 2004).

6. *Branded Nation*

7. Chuck Kent, president, Creative On Call, e-mail communication with the author, October 5, 2005.

8. "A brand is a promise" is credited to David Aakar, vice-chairman of Prophet, a leading brand-consulting firm.

9. Shaun Smith and Joe Wheeler, *Managing the Customer Experience: Turning Customers into Advocates*

(London: Prentice-Hall, Financial Times, 2002).

10. Colin Shaw and John Ivens, *Building Great Customer Experiences* (Basingstoke, UK: Palgrave Macmillan, 2002).

11. Rolf Jensen, *The Dream Society: How the Coming Shift from Information to Imagination Will Transform Your Business* (New York: McGraw Hill, 1999).

12. Knapp and Sherwin, *Destination BrandScience*.

13. Nissan Pathfinder 2006 e-brochure, downloaded from www.nissanusa.com.

14. Klein, *No Logo*.

15. www.merriam-webstercollegiate.com.

16. *Built to Last*

17. Klein, *No Logo*; *Branded Nation*.

18. *Branded Nation*

19. Klein, *No Logo*.

20. *The Corporation*. DVD, produced and directed by Mark Achbar, Jennifer Abbott, and Joel Bakan. 2 hr., 25 min. (Zeitgeist Films, 2003); Klein, *No Logo*.

21. Thomas L. Friedman, *The World Is Flat: A Brief History of the Twenty-First Century* (New York: Farrar, Straus and Giroux, 2005).

22. Marcus Kabel, "Wal-Mart Plans to Sell More Organic Merchandise," *San Diego Union-Tribune*, March 25, 2006.

23. California State Parks press release, May 26, 2005.

24. *Citizen Brand*

25. Tatyana Sizonenko-Leventhal, "Remolding the Museum's Image Through Branding: Benefits and Challenges Associated with Branding in San Francisco Bay Area Museums" (master's thesis, John F. Kennedy University, Pleasant Hill, Calif.: 2003).

26. Sabina Carr, "An Urban Oasis: A Branding Success Story" (PowerPoint presentation at the annual meeting of the American Association of Botanical Gardens and Arboreta, Dallas, June 2004).

27. David Nicandri, "The Walls Talk," *Museum News* November–December 2005. Admissions went up 17.3 percent and donations doubled in the first year after rebranding.

28. *Emotional Branding*

29. Jon Schallert, president, the Schallert Group, telephone communication with the author, April 7, 2006; www.jonschallert.com.

30. Mark Rudzinski and Linda Wilson, "Segmentation Studies and Their Application" (PowerPoint presentation at the annual meeting of the Visitor Studies Association, Albuquerque, N.M., August 2004).

31. Linda Wilson, manager of audience research and evaluation for the Shedd Aquarium, e-mail communication with the author, July 27, 2005.

32. John Falk, "The Impact of Visit Motivation on Learning: Using Identity As a Construct to Understand the Visitor Experience," *Curator* 49, no. 2 (2006). See the download from www.aza.org/ConEd/mirp/. This ILI research was funded by the National Science Foundation in collaboration with the Association for Zoos and Aquariums.

33. Michael McKechnie, "The ABC's of Branding Your Organization" (PowerPoint presentation at the annual meeting of the American Association of Botanical Gardens and Arboreta, Dallas, June 2004). Having to incorporate a donor's or sponsor's name in your institution's name can create an unnecessary challenge to remain successful long after opening day, which greatly dilutes the impact of a generous donation. In San Diego, the Reuben H. Fleet Science Center is often shortened to the Fleet Science Center. The name "Fleet" suggests airplanes and flight, which usually blends well with their subject matter. But it also causes confusion for visitors to San Diego's Balboa Park, where the San Diego Air and Space Museum is just a short walk away. Chicago's Academy of Sciences became the Peggy S. Notebaert Nature Museum. They still struggle with their name. If they had become simply the Nature Museum things would have been clearer for their audience. Sometimes the name is a mismatch with the subject matter, as in the Birch Aquarium, La Jolla, California, named for donor Stephen Birch.

Chapter 6

1. Scott Davis, "Taking Control of Your Brand's Destiny," *Brandweek*, October 15, 2001, quoted in *Citizen Brand*.

2. *Fabled Service*

3. *Built to Last*

4. *Citizen Brand*

5. Robert Spector and Patrick D. McCarthy, *The Nordstrom Way: The Inside Story of America's #1 Customer Service Company* (New York: John Wiley and Sons, 2000).

6. *Nuts!*

7. *Guts!*

8. *Be Our Guest*

9. *Built to Last*

10. *Guts!*

11. Colin Shaw and John Ivens, *Building Great Customer Experiences* (Basingstoke, UK: Palgrave Macmillan, 2002).

12. Ibid.

13. Kevin Blessing, general manager, Central Market, interview with the author, May 26, 2006.

14. *Guts!*

15. Bill Capodagli and Lynn Jackson, *The Disney Way: Harnessing the Management Secrets of Disney in Your Company* (New York: McGraw Hill, 1999).

16. *Built to Last*

17. Peter C. Honebein and Roy F. Cammarano, *Creating Do-It-Yourself Customers: How Great Customer Experiences Build Great Companies* (Mason, Ohio: Thomson, 2005).

18. *Fabled Service*

19. Shaw and Ivens, *Building Great Customer Experiences*.

20. Don Buckley, librarian, Cerritos Public Library, telephone interview with the author, November 2, 2006.

21. Jakob Nielsen, "10 Best Intranets of 2005," *Alertbox*, January 26, 2006; www.useit.com.

22. *Fabled Service*. Sixty-eight percent of customers who leave companies are turned off by an attitude of indifference on the part of a company employee.

23. *Guts!*

24. Spector and McCarthy, *Nordstrom Way*.

25. *Nuts!*

26. *Guts!*

27. Timothy R. Hinken and J. Bruce Tracey, "Development and Use of a Web-Based Tool to Measure the Costs of Employee Turnover: Preliminary Findings," *CHR Reports*, May 2006 (downloaded from www.chr.cornell. edu). A free turnover-costs calculator is available at www.chr.cornell.edu under "Tools for the Hospitality Industry." While the tool was developed for hotels and restaurants, anyone is welcome to use it.

28. Aspen Institute Domestic Strategy Group, *Grow Faster Together or Grow Slowly Apart: How Will America Work in the 21st Century?* (downloaded in pdf format from www.aspeninstitute.org, ISBN: 0-89843-356-8). The projections change each year, but experts agree that a skilled-worker shortage could be widespread as soon as 2010. Companies are already reporting problems finding skilled sales representatives, engineers, and technicians. "Manpower Survey Shows Worldwide 'Talent Shortage,'" *Yahoo News*, February 20, 2006). For up-to-date information, visit www.bls.gov.

29. Michael Kinsman, "Baby Boomer Exodus: As Millions Retire, Their Skills and Knowledge Will Be Gone, Too," *San Diego Union-Tribune*, April 23, 2006.

30. Michael Brill and Sue Weidemann, *Disproving Widespread Myths About Workplace Design* (Buffalo, N.Y.: Kimball International, 2001).

31. Tony Hiss, *The Experience of Place: A New Way of Looking at and Dealing with Our Radically Changing Cities and Countryside* (New York: Knopf, 1990), quotes BOSTI research; www.bosti.com.

32. Brill and Weidemann, *Disproving Widespread Myths*.

33. The landmark study was conducted in the 1950s by psychologists Abraham Maslow and Norbett Mintz. Cited in Hiss, *Experience of Place.*

34. Brill and Weidemann, *Disproving Widespread Myths.*

35. Nielsen, "10 Best Intranets of 2005."

36. Ibid.

Chapter 7

1. Sean Adams and Noreen Morioka, *Logo Design Workbook: A Hands-on Guide to Creating Logos* (Gloucester, Mass.: Rockport Publishers, 2004).

2. Duane Knapp and Gary Sherwin, *Destination BrandScience* (Washington, D.C.: International Association of Convention and Visitors Bureaus, 2005).

3. Colin Shaw and John Ivens, *Building Great Customer Experiences* (Basingstoke, UK: Palgrave Macmillan, 2002). This is the definitive book on call centers, with many great ideas on how to make them more cost effective while improving your customer experience.

4. Marilyn Hood, "Staying Away: Why People Choose Not to Visit Museums," in *Reinventing the Museum: Historical and Contemporary Perspectives on the Paradigm Shift*, ed. Gail Anderson (Walnut Creek, Calif.: AltaMira Press, 2004); first published in *Museum News*, April 1983. Steven Yalowitz, audience research specialist, Monterey Bay Aquarium, telephone conversation with the author, July 19, 2005.

5. Adams and Morioka, *Logo Design Workbook.*

6. Knapp and Sherwin, *Destination BrandScience.*

7. Tanya Bredehoft, principal, Artefact Design, e-mail communication with the author, March 6, 2006; www.purecorn.com.

8. Adams and Morioka, *Logo Design Workbook*.

9. Sheila Jackson, assistant director, Carnegie Library, telephone interview with the author, November 16, 2006.

10. *Call of the Mall*

11. Mitzi Sims, *Sign Design: Graphics, Materials, Techniques* (New York: Van Nostrand Reinhold, 1991).

12. *Why We Buy*

Chapter 8

1. *With People in Mind*

2. *Why We Buy*

3. Kathleen Wolf, "Business District Streetscapes, Trees, and Consumer Response," *Journal of Forestry* 103, no. 8 (December 2005). Depending on the size of the city, respondents said they would spend nine to twelve percent more at businesses with trees out front.

4. Martin M. Pegler, *Streetscapes* (New York: Retail Reporting Corporation, 1998).

5. *Why We Buy*

6. Evan Terry Associates, ed., *Pocket Guide to the ADA* (New York: John Wiley and Sons, 1997).

7. *Why We Buy*

8. Motoo Nakonishi, *Corporate Design Systems: Identity Through Graphics* (New York: PBC International, 1985).

9. David Ausubel, *Educational Psychology: A Cognitive View.* (New York: Rinehart and Winston, 1968), quoted in John W. Coffey and Alberto J. Cañas, "An Advance Organizer Approach to Distance Learning Course Presentation." (Proceedings of the Nineteenth International Conference on Technology and Education, Tallahassee, Fla., May 2–5, 2001.)

10. *Chocolate, The Exhibition* was developed by Chicago's Field Museum of Natural History, www.fieldmuseum.org.

11. *Learning from Museums*

12. Deborah Jacobs, city librarian, Seattle Public Library, telephone interview with the author, November 20, 2006.

13. M. Cristina Medina, "Aquarium Reaches Out to Latinos," www.montereyherald.com, June 25, 2005.

Chapter 9

1. *With People in Mind.* Al Shacklett, "Circulation Design to Enhance the Visitor Experience," *Public Garden* 19, no. 4 (2004).

2. *Why We Buy.* Paco Underhill is a pioneer in "retail anthropology," the study of how people behave in stores. He and his team at Envirosell (www.envirosell.com) discovered the concept of the transition zone during their twenty years of work. It is also mentioned in his second book, *The Call of the Mall.* All the information about the transition zone comes from him.

3. Ibid.

4. *Psychology of the Consumer.* Also found in Wayne Hunt, *Environmental Graphics: Projects & Process* (New York: Harper Design International, 2003).

5. *Why We Buy*

6. Sheila Jackson, assistant director, Carnegie Library, telephone interview with the author, November 16, 2006.

7. *With People in Mind*

8. Ibid; Lisa Brochu, *Interpretive Planning: The 5-M Model for Successful Planning Projects* (Fort Collins, Colo.: Interp Press, 2003).

9. *Call of the Mall*

10. *With People in Mind*

11. Hunt, *Environmental Graphics.*

12. *Why We Buy*

13. Deborah Jacobs, city librarian, Seattle Public Library, telephone interview with the author, November 20, 2006.

14. *With People in Mind.* Our "channel capacity," the space in our brains to hold certain kinds of information, maxes out at seven, in Malcolm Gladwell, *The Tipping Point: How Little Things Make a Big Difference* (Boston: Little, Brown and Company, 2000).

15. Hunt, *Environmental Graphics.*

16. *Why We Buy*

17. *Psychology of the Consumer*; Hunt, *Environmental Graphics.*

18. *Why We Buy*

19. Ibid.

20. Kathryn Owen, audience research coordinator, Woodland Park Zoo, e-mail communication with the author, March 22, 2006.

Chapter 10

1. *Call of the Mall*

2. Frank Green, "More Malls Cozying Up to Visitors: Stores Hope Shoppers Will Feel at Home, Spend More," *San Diego Union-Tribune*, April 26, 2006.

3. Don Peppers and Martha Rogers, *Enterprise One to One: Tools for Competing in the Interactive Age* (New York: Currency Books, 1997). This book helps businesses understand the value of individual customers.

4. *Psychology of the Consumer*

5. *Call of the Mall*

6. The Morton Arboretum did some visitor studies before opening its new children's garden, and even put up signs to let parents know that the toilets were not auto-flush.

7. Deborah Jacobs, city librarian, Seattle Public Library, telephone interview with the author, November 20, 2006.

8. Ibid.

9. *Psychology of the Consumer*; *Branded Nation*

10. Hannah Weisman, "Something for Everyone: Visitor Services in Art Museums" (master's thesis, State University of New York at Oneonta, 2004).

11. *Psychology of the Consumer*. The notion of "effort vs. reward" related to museum signage is discussed at length by interpretive signage expert Dave Bucy in his "Planning for Success" workshop. (Presentation at the annual meeting of the National Association for Interpretation, Anchorage, Alaska, October 1998.)

12. *Psychology of the Consumer*

13. *With People in Mind*

14. Paul Orselli, "Good Things Come in Small Packages," *Exhibitionist* 24, no. 1 (Spring 2005).

15. Malcolm Gladwell, *The Tipping Point: How Little Things Make a Big Difference* (Boston: Little, Brown and Company, 2000). The "broken-window theory" is also mentioned in Wayne Hunt, *Environmental Graphics: Projects & Process* (New York: Harper Design International, 2003).

16. Deborah Jacobs, city librarian, Seattle Public Library, telephone interview with the author, November 20, 2006.

17. Bruce Thurston, associate director of facilities, San Diego Zoo, e-mail communication with the author, April 19, 2006.

18. *Learning from Museums*

19. *With People in Mind*

20. Sonya Fauré, *Hideaways: Cabins, Huts, and Tree House Escapes* (Paris: Éditions Flammarion, 2004).

21. Jay Appleton, *The Experience of Landscape* (New York: John Wiley and Sons, 1975), quoted by Kathryn Owen, audience research coordinator, Woodland Park Zoo, e-mail communication with the author, March 14, 2006.

22. Faith Popcorn, "Faith Popcorn's Predictions for 2005— Choice Without Challenge," www.faithpopcorn.com (December 2004).

23. www.nowandnext.com (August 2005).

24. Toyota Camry ad in *Newsweek*, May 29, 2006.

25. Kate Washington, "The Power of One," *Sunset* (April 2005). In San Diego, Urban Grind Coffeehouse provides make-your-own-S'mores desserts, while Spread Restaurant's entire menu is based on gourmet peanut butter.

Chapter 11

1. *Psychology of the Consumer*

2. Creating a theme is similar to creating a "Big Idea" for an exhibition. See Beverly Serrell, *Exhibit Labels: An Interpretive Approach* (Walnut Creek, Calif.: AltaMira Press, 1996).

3. *Be Our Guest*

4. Larry Beck, "'Wicked' Interpretation: Lessons from Broadway," *The Interpreter* 1, no. 4 (July–August 2005).

5. John Gatewood and Catherine Cameron, "Battlefield Pilgrims at Gettysburg National Military Park," *Ethnology* 43, no. 3 (Summer 2004).

6. The concept of the "Big Idea" is from Beverly Serrell's marvelous book *Exhibit Labels*. Serrell developed the concept specifically to improve the quality and cohesiveness of interpretive texts for museum exhibitions. It's an invaluable resource for anyone writing for exhibitions.

7. *Be Our Guest*

8. Sheila Jackson, assistant director, Carnegie Library, telephone interview with the author, November 16, 2006, and Deborah Jacobs, city librarian, Seattle Public Library, telephone interview with the author, November 20, 2006.

9. Serrell, *Exhibit Labels*.

10. Troy Cooper, president and COO, Rockfish Seafood Grill, telephone interview with the author, April 17, 2006.

11. Mix in a few labels at a ninth- or tenth-grade level.

Readability is based on the length of sentences and the difficulty of words. Shorter sentences give a higher readability score. The criticism of labels written at a lower grade level and with higher readability is that museums are "dumbing down" content. Your audience may be capable of reading at a twelfth-grade or college level. But people don't want to walk around a museum and read a "textbook" posted on a wall. Grade level and readability are measures of comfort; they make your content accessible. Would you rather have many visitors reading most of your labels, or just a few visitors reading them all?

12. The minimum typeface for the main text on signs should be 18 pt. This is another reason why good signs are brief.

13. Robin Williams, *The Non-Designer's Design Book: Design and Typographic Principles for the Visual Novice*, 2nd Edition (Berkeley, Calif.: Peachpit Press, 2004).

14. *Why We Buy*

15. A few signs will end up longer, but it's a good rule of thumb for visitor-centered interpretation. The "chunking" concept comes from George Miller's 1956 essay, "The Magical Number 7, Plus or Minus 2," referred to in Sam H. Ham, *Environmental Interpretation: A Practical Guide for People with Big Ideas and Small Budgets* (Golden, Colo.: Fulcrum Publishing, 1992) as well as in Malcolm Gladwell, *The Tipping Point: How Little Things Make a Big Difference* (Boston: Little, Brown and Company, 2000).

16. *Psychology of the Consumer*

17. Douglas M. Knutson, Ted T. Cable, and Larry Beck, *Interpretation of Cultural and Natural Resources* (State College, Pa.: Venture Publishing, 1995).

18. This process is adapted from Serrell's *Exhibit Labels*.

19. Beverly Serrell, *Paying Attention: Visitors and Museum Exhibitions* (Washington, D.C.: American Association of Museums, 1998).

20. Williams, *Non-Designer's Design Book*.

21. Ham, *Environmental Interpretation*.

22. Thanks to researcher Dave Bucy for introducing me to the chunking concept at the "Planning for Success" workshop at the annual meeting of the National Association of Interpretation, Anchorage, Alaska, October 1998.

23. *Psychology of the Consumer*

24. See Nancy Owens Renner, "The Bilingual Dilemma: Should We or Shouldn't We?" *Exhibitionist* 22, no.

1 (Spring 2003) and "Taking the Bilingual Leap" *Exhibitionist* 22, no. 2 (Fall 2003), available on www.experienceology.com.

25. Lynn Baxter, "Multilingual Signs—The Future?" *Identity* September–October 1996.

26. T. Scott Gross, *Outrageous! Unforgettable Service . . . Guilt-free Selling* (New York: American Management Association, 1998).

27. Mary Kay Cunningham, *The Interpreters Training Manual for Museums*. (Washington, D.C.: American Association of Museums, 2004).

28. Gladwell, *Tipping Point*.

Chapter 12

1. Tom Kelley, *The Art of Innovation: Lessons in Creativity from IDEO, America's Leading Design Firm* (New York: Currency Books, 2001).

2. *Nuts!*

3. *Citizen Brand*

4. *Learning from Museums*

5. Deborah Perry and Kris Morrissey, e-mail communication with the author, November 14, 2005.

6. John H. Falk and Lynn D. Dierking, *Lessons Without Limit: How Free-Choice Learning Is Transforming Education* (Walnut Creek, Calif.: AltaMira Press, 2002).

7. Minda Borun et al., *Family Learning in Museums: The PISEC Perspective* (Philadelphia: PISEC, 1998), quoted in Sandy Tanck, "The Perennial Photosynthesis Challenge," *Public Garden* 19, no. 1 (2004).

8. Gianna Moscardo, *Making Visitors Mindful: Principles for Creating Sustainable Visitor Experiences Through Effective Communication* (Champaign, Ill.: Sagamore Publishing, 1999).

9. Falk and Dierking, *Lessons Without Limit*.

10. Martin Lindstrom, *Brand Sense: Build Powerful Brands Through Touch, Taste, Smell, Sight, and Sound* (New York: Free Press, 2005).

11. Sheila Jackson, assistant director, Carnegie Library, telephone interview with the author, November 16, 2006.

12. *Why We Buy*

13. Ibid.

14. Try www.internetapollo.com to get started.

15. Libby Quaid, "Wines with Animal Pictures on Labels Hot Sellers," *San Diego Union-Tribune*, March 18, 2006.

16. *Why We Buy*

17. Lindstrom, *Brand Sense*; Malcolm Gladwell, *Blink: The Power of Thinking Without Thinking* (New York: Little, Brown and Company, 2005).

18. Moscardo, *Making Visitors Mindful*.

19. *Be Our Guest*

20. Lindstrom, *Brand Sense*.

21. Ibid.

22. *Psychology of the Consumer*

23. Ibid.

24. Lindstrom, *Brand Sense*.

25. www.holosonics.com. Audio Spotlight speakers (complete with amplifiers) are $2,000 to $2,500, depending on size. Volume discounts are available.

26. *Be Our Guest*

27. *Why We Buy*

28. www.scentair.com/scentbranding/index. cfm?subSectionID=1.

29. *Be Our Guest*

30. *Emotional Branding*

31. *Why We Buy*; Lindstrom, *Brand Sense*.

32. Emma Hunt, marketing manager, JORVIK Viking Centre, e-mail communication with the author, May 10, 2006; www.jorvik-viking-centre.co.uk.

33. Both Febreze and Glade Plug-Ins offer inexpensive scent options in the U.S. However, the products aren't guaranteed to be oil free, which is essential for merchandise and museum locations. Scent solutions vented through an HVAC system are available through www.aromasys.com. These are used in the hospitality and gaming industries. Other companies—www. prolitec.com, www.scentair.com, www.aerome. com, www.scentcommunication.com, and Escential Resources—provide dry aerosol systems that can be narrowly targeted for point-of-sale or single-room applications. These oil-free technologies are safe to use with merchandise or in museums.

34. *Be Our Guest*

35. Lindstrom, *Brand Sense*.

36. *Why We Buy*

37. Check out www.sweets.construction.com and look at all the vendors under "Finishes." Pirelli Flooring makes fun bumpy plastics. For amazing 3-D models from satellite imagery, try www.stm-usa.com. For skulls and other nature-related items, try www.acornnaturalists. com or www.carolina.com.

38. *Be Our Guest*

39. Ibid.

40. T. Scott Gross, *Positively Outrageous Service: New & Easy Ways to Win Customers for Life* (New York: Mastermedia Limited, 1991).

41. *Experience Economy*

Chapter 13

1. David F. D'Alessandro, *Brand Warfare: 10 Rules for Building the Killer Brand* (New York: McGraw Hill, 2001).

2. *Be Our Guest*

3. Sylvia Hui, "Hong Kong Disneyland Is Feng Shui Adventure," *San Diego Union-Tribune*, September 18, 2005.

4. Colin Shaw and John Ivens, *Building Great Customer Experiences* (Basingstoke, UK: Palgrave Macmillan, 2002).

5. *Built to Last*

6. Wayne Hunt, *Environmental Graphics: Projects & Process* (New York: Harper Design International, 2003).

7. Deborah Jacobs, city librarian, Seattle Public Library, telephone interview with the author, November 20, 2006.

8. Chip Bell and Bilijack Bell, *Magnetic Service: Secrets for Creating Passionately Devoted Customers* (San Francisco: Berrett-Kohler, 2003).

9. Charles Fishman, "Space Shot: You Wish You Worked Here—Georgia Aquarium," *Fast Company*, December 2006–January 2007.

10. Try these Web sites to get you started: www. nowandnext.com and www.trendwatching.com. For branding trends see www.martinlindstrom.com. For trends within the environmental education community, visit www.biodiversityproject.org.

11. *Why We Buy*; www.envirosell.com.

12. Joe Ilvento and Doug Price, *License to Serve: Beyond Selling ... The How-To Guide for Creating Exceptional Customer Service* (West Long Branch, N.J.: Applied Business Communications, 2004).

13. Bell and Bell, *Magnetic Service*.

14. A thorough description of this technique is found in Beverly Serrell, *Paying Attention: Visitors and Museum Exhibitions* (Washington, D.C.: American Association of Museums, 1998).

15. Madeleine Pullman and Stephani Robson, "A Picture Is Worth a Thousand Words: Using Photo-Elicitation to

Solicit Hotel Guests' Feedback," *CHR Tool No. 7—Tools for the Hospitality Industry*, Cornell University School of Hotel Administration—The Center for Hospitality Research. Available from www.chr.cornell.edu. You can use www.flickr.com for free uploads, creating a private group just for your staff and the visitors you invite to give feedback.

16. Gianna Moscardo, *Making Visitors Mindful: Principles for Creating Sustainable Visitor Experiences Through Effective Communication* (Champaign, Ill.: Sagamore Publishing, 1999).

17. Cia Romano, principal, Interface Guru, presentation to the San Diego Evaluators and Exhibits Group, February 22, 2006; www.interfaceguru.com.

18. Melissa Maynard, "Picture This," *Hour Detroit*, May 2006.

19. Susan Greenstein, "Who Goes There? The Importance of Doing and Using Visitor Research," *Public Garden* 19, no. 2 (2004).

20. *Emotional Branding*. In *The Experience Economy* Pine and Gilmore talk at length about the need for companies to customize their products, producing them in response to an individual consumer's desires.

21. "In Brief," *Museum News*, July–August 2005.

22. Randy Kennedy, "With Irreverence and an iPod, Recreating the Museum Tour," *New York Times*, May 28, 2005. Julia Beizer, "The Pods Have Landed," *Museum News*, September–October 2005.

23. Kirk Carter Mona, "Pushing Boundaries: Eight Keys to a Successful Outreach Program," *The Interpreter*, July–August 2005.

24. Robert Weller, "Resorts Tame Slopes for Older Folks," *San Diego Union-Tribune*, November 6, 2005.

25. Ilvento and Price, *License to Serve*.

26. Mark O'Neill, "The Social Obligation of Museums." (Presentation at a meeting of the Museum Educators of Southern California, Los Angeles, October 2003.) Available on www.experienceology.com.

27. John H. Falk and Lynn D. Dierking, *Lessons Without Limit: How Free-Choice Learning Is Transforming Education* (Walnut Creek, Calif.: AltaMira Press, 2002).

28. David Mininberg, Nancy Thompson, and Joseph Fins, "The Art of Medicine at the Metropolitan Museum of Art"; Marcia Semmes, "Vital Visionaries: The Museum Cure," *Museum News*, May–June 2005.

29. Diana Allen and Terry Eastin, "Rollin' and Strollin':

The Arkansas River Trail Experience," *Legacy* 16, no. 4 (July–August 2005).

30. *Citizen Brand*

31. Ibid.

32. Reinier Evers, "Being Spaces & Brand Spaces," *Trend Briefing*, March 2006; www.trendwatching.com.

33. *Citizen Brand*

34. Susan Breitkopf, "M Notes: Historic Site's Fright Nights," *Museum News*, September–October 2004.

35. Ellen R. Stapleton, "Some Museums Allow Yoga Enthusiasts to Work out in Artistic Atmosphere," www.nctimes.com, July 5, 2006.

36. John Chiodo, "Out of the United States of Mind," *The Exhibitionist* 23, no. 2 (Fall 2004).

37. Katie Coldwell, "Star of the Month: Greg Miller," *Southwest Airlines Spirit*, April 2006.

38. Evers, "Being Spaces."

Chapter 14

1. Donna Walker, co-owner, South Bark Dog Wash, personal communication with the author, September 14, 2005.

2. Robert McKee, *Story: Substance, Structure, Style, and the Principles of Screenwriting* (New York: ReganBooks, 1997).

3. Russell W. Belk, "Been There, Done That, Bought the Souvenirs: Of Journeys and Boundary Crossing," in *Consumer Research: Postcards from the Edge*, eds. S. Brown and D. Turley (London: Routledge, 1997).

4. Joe Ilvento and Doug Price, *License to Serve: Beyond Selling … The How-To Guide for Creating Exceptional Customer Service* (West Long Branch, N.J.: Applied Business Communications, 2004).

5. Jon Schallert, president, the Schallert Group, telephone communication with the author, April 7, 2006; www.jonschallert.com.

6. Godfrey Evans, *Souvenirs: From Roman Times to the Present Day* (Edinburgh: NMS Publishing, 1999). Unless otherwise noted, all the information in this section comes from this lovely book.

7. Michael Houlihan, "Souvenirs with Soul: 800 Years of Pilgrimage to Santiago de Compostela," in *Souvenirs: The Material Culture of Tourism*, eds. Michael Hitchcock and Ken Teague (Aldershot, UK: Ashgate Publishing, 2000).

8. W.B. Hansen and I. Altman, "Decorating Personal Places: A Descriptive Analysis," *Environment and*

Behavior 8 (December 1976).

9. Stephanie A. Clemons, James H. Banning, and David A. McKelfresh, "The Importance of Sense of Place and Sense of Self in Residence Hall Room Design," *Journal of Student Affairs* 8 (2004).

10. Russell W. Belk, professor, University of Utah, e-mail communication with the author, May 13, 2006.

11. Russell W. Belk, Melanie Wallendorf, John F. Sherry, Jr., "The Sacred and the Profane in Consumer Behavior: Theodicy on the Odyssey," *Journal of Consumer Research* 16 (June 1989).

12. Russell W. Belk, professor, University of Utah, e-mail communication with the author, May 13, 2006.

13. Troy Cooper, president and COO, Rockfish Seafood Grill, telephone interview with the author, April 17, 2006.

14. Stacey Menzel Baker, Susan Schultz Kleine, and Heather E. Bowen, "On the Symbolic Meanings of Souvenirs for Children," *Research in Consumer Behavior* 10 (2006).

15. Mihaly Csikszentmihayli and Eugene Rochberg-Halton, *The Meaning of Things: Domestic Symbols and the Self* (Cambridge: Cambridge University Press, 1981).

16. Russell W. Belk, Melanie Wallendorf, John F. Sherry, Jr., and Morris B. Holbrook, "Collecting in a Consumer Culture," in *Highways and Buyways: Naturalistic Research from the Consumer Behavior Odyssey*, ed. Russell W. Belk (Provo, Utah: Association for Consumer Research, 1991).

17. Preston Turegano, "Pay to Play: For a Nice Contribution, Donors Get Perks Aplenty at San Diego's Arts Organizations," *San Diego Union-Tribune*, February 12, 2006.

18. *Philadelphia Stories: A Collection of Pivotal Museum Memories.* VHS tape, produced and edited by Michael Spock. 60 min. (Exhibit Media, 2000).

19. Baker et al., "On the Symbolic Meanings of Souvenirs for Children."

20. Belk et al., "Collecting in a Consumer Culture."

21. Ibid.

22. Beverly Gordon, "Souvenir: Messenger of the Extraordinary," *Journal of Popular Culture* 20, no. 3 (1986).

23. This numbering system is mine, not Gordon's. It is based on my best guess, from my research and personal experience, of which items are likely to be kept the longest.

24. *Branded Nation*

25. Belk et al., "Sacred and the Profane."

26. John F. Sherry, Jr., "The Soul of the Company Store: Nike Town Chicago and the Emplaced Brandscape," in *ServiceScapes: The Concept of Place in Contemporary Markets*, ed. John F. Sherry, Jr. (Chicago: NTC Business Books, 1998).

27. Lisa Brochu, *Interpretive Planning: The 5-M Model for Successful Planning Projects* (Fort Collins, Colo.: Interp Press, 2003).

28. Tanya Bredehoft, principal, Artefact Design, personal communication with the author, February 15, 2006; www.purecorn.com.

29. *Branded Nation*

30. Patrick Thorne, "Outside In," *Hemispheres*, May 2006.

31. Melissa Nelson, "They Hope That 'Armani-Style Fishing' Will Suit Women," *San Diego Union-Tribune*, July 2, 2006.

INDEX